The Origins of Things

(or how the hour got its minutes)

D1468813

Library of Congress Cataloging-in-Publication Data

The Origins of Things: Or How the Hour Got Its Minutes
Contributors, Alan L. Boegehold...[et al]; editor, Jack Meinhardt

1. Mesopotamia—inventions. 2. Egypt—inventions.
3. Greece—Rome—inventions.
4. Ancient world—technology. 5. Ancient world—institutions.
6. Ancient world—science.
I. Alan L. Boegehold. II. Jack Meinhardt. III. Archaeology Odyssey magazine.

© 2002 Biblical Archaeology Society
4710 41st St., NW
Washington, DC 20016

Design by Frank Sheehan
ISBN 1-880317-60-5

The Origins of Things
(or how the hour got its minutes)

—*Contributors*—

Alan L. Boegehold	Alexander Jones
Harold Brodsky	Samuel Kurinsky
J. Harold Ellens	Leonora Neville
George B. Griffenhagen	Rush Rehm
William W. Hallo	Timothy Rogers
Michael Hudson	Denise Schmandt-Besserat
Kim Jonas	James Sickinger

—*Editor*—
Jack Meinhardt

BIBLICAL ARCHAEOLOGY SOCIETY • WASHINGTON, D.C.

Table of Contents

The Mediterranean World

Acknowledgments

The Biblical Archaeology Society would like to thank the editors, both past and present, who helped put together the Origins columns in *Archaeology Odyssey* : Allison Dickens, Sudip Bose, Lindsey Todd, Jessica Meyerson, Julia Bozzolo and Nancy Lewis. We would also like to thank Frank Sheehan, who designed this book, and David Clark, whose whimsical drawing graces its cover.

Foreword

The origins of Origins, a series of short articles published in *Archaeology Odyssey* magazine, is a tale in itself.

In 1997 Hershel Shanks, editor of *Biblical Archaeology Review* and *Bible Review*, decided to launch a third journal. Working on magazines devoted to the Bible and the biblical period, we editors were always coming across civilizations that were sometimes familiar but more often very strange; for every Egyptian, Greek and Roman, there was an Urukian, Luwian and Commagene. Hershel's idea was to publish a magazine devoted to all these circumambient peoples—the world around the Bible, so to speak. It was thrilling to think that this new magazine, *Archaeology Odyssey*, along with the biblical magazines, would deal with the main tributaries of Western civilization.

Creating a magazine is more than a matter of gathering material and publishing it. A good magazine is almost an organism; it has a heart, blood, lungs, muscle and a funny bone. The more I thought about the look and feel—the personality—of the magazine, the more important it seemed to me that we deal directly with the idea of time, that is, with the relation between the time-past of the ancient world and our time-present. If the past were simply dead and gone, why would anyone in her right mind make the effort (or fork out the cash) to read *Archaeology Odyssey*?

The answer, of course, is that the past, even the most remote past, is not just defunct. Like forms of life, some cultures and civilizations go extinct, having no influence on the course of history. But even in this case the past is not just dead and gone; indeed, to learn about influenceless peoples is to learn something about human possibility—not about who we are, but about who we are not but might have been.

And then there is that other case, in which the past continues to co-exist with us, though we are largely unaware of its presence. Thus Origins.

Some years earlier I had read Daniel Boorstin's book *The Discoverers* (1983). In Boorstin's fascinating discussion of clocks, I learned that our 60-minute hour owes its existence to the ancient Babylonians. Imagine that! A counting system in use 4,000 years ago is responsible for the design of the watch on my wrist. Here, then, was an idea for a department in *Archaeology Odyssey*: a column tracing ideas, technologies or institutions—especially ideas we tend to take for granted—that had their beginnings in the ancient world covered in the magazine. We'd call it "Origins."

I then learned that William W. Hallo, the William M. Laffan Professor of Assyriology and Babylonian Literature at Yale University (and a member of *Archaeology Odyssey*'s Editorial Advisory Board), had recently published a book called *Origins: The Ancient Near Eastern Background of Some Modern Western*

Institutions (Brill, 1996). In his introduction, Hallo writes that he, too, was inspired by *The Discoverers*, especially Boorstin's description of "humanity's dawning awareness of the world around it, and its ceaseless efforts to organize its observations into an intelligible system." Hallo then decided to write a history of the ancient Near Eastern roots of certain Western ideas, technologies and institutions.

Origins the column became linked to *Origins* the book when Bill Hallo agreed to write about the development of the calendar for *Archaeology Odyssey*—"In One Era and Out the Other," the very first Origins column and the first chapter in this book.

Now, after five years of publishing Origins columns in every other issue of *Archaeology Odyssey*, five years of watching early humanity discovering the outside world and disciplining its discoveries in science and art, we have decided to assemble them together in a book. This book is meant to be enjoyable, but its chapters are written by scholars. We want to inform you by pleasing you, as Alexander Pope said of the purpose of poetry. I hope you have as much fun reading the book as I had editing it—and I hope to see you again in five years!

Jack Meinhardt
Managing Editor
ARCHAEOLOGY ODYSSEY

Contributors

Alan L. Boegehold is a professor of classics at Brown University.

Harold Brodsky is an associate professor in the Department of Geography at the University of Maryland. He is writing a textbook on the geography of the Hebrew Bible.

J. Harold Ellens is a research scholar at the University of Michigan and an occasional lecturer at Claremont Graduate School in California.

George B. Griffenhagen is a pharmacist and former curator of the Smithsonian Institution's division of medical sciences.

William W. Hallo is the William M. Laffan Professor of Assyriology and Babylonian Literature at Yale University and curator of its Babylonian Collection.

Michael Hudson is a research associate in Babylonian economic development at Harvard's Peabody Museum and president of the Institute for the Development of Long Term Economic Trends.

Kim Jonas, a former college math professor, is currently a statistician for the U.S. Census Bureau.

Alexander Jones is a professor of classics at the University of Toronto.

Samuel Kurinsky is the author of *The Glassmakers* (Hippocrene Books, 1991).

Leonora Neville is an assistant professor of Byzantine history at Catholic University in Washington, D.C.

Rush Rehm is an associate professor of Drama and Classics at Stanford University.

Timothy Rogers is a rare-books scholar and a lecturer in the Department of English at Furman University in South Carolina.

Denise Schmandt-Besserat, a professor of Middle Eastern Studies at the University of Texas at Austin, is the author of *How Writing Came About* (1996).

James Sickinger is an associate professor of classics at Florida State University.

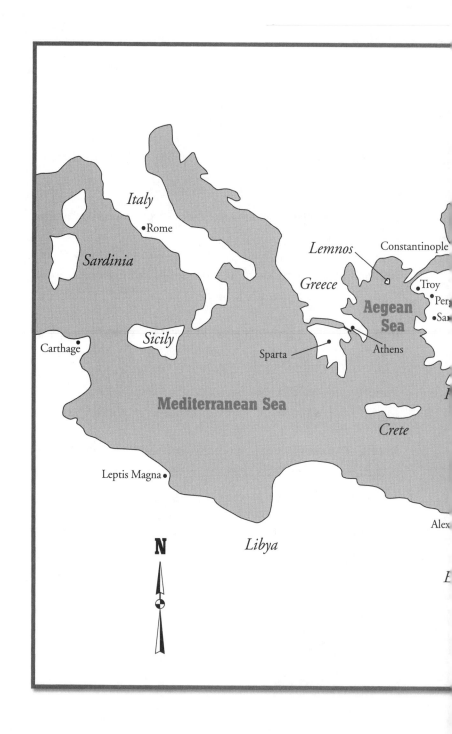

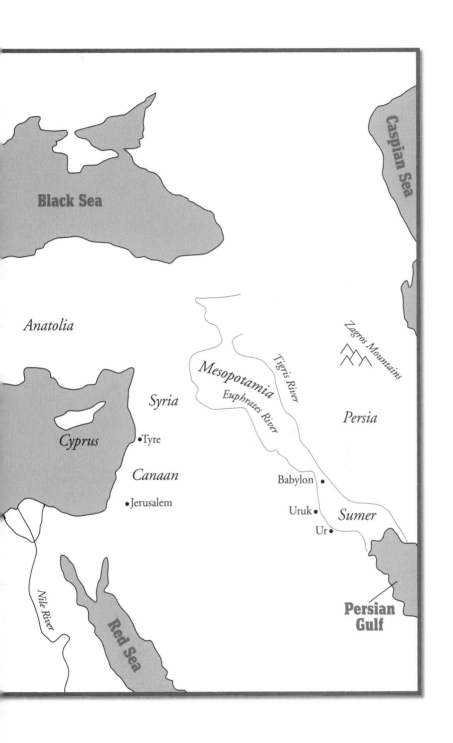

In One Era and Out the Other

William W. Hallo

Did the new millennium begin on January 1, 2000, or, since there was never a year called 0, on January 1, 2001 (that is, 2000 years after the year 1)? Should it be called 2000 A.D. (*Anno Domini*, Latin for "in the year of the Lord") or A.D. 2000? Or 2000 C.E. (for "Common Era")?

Why is it 2000 anyway? Two thousand years after what? The birth of Christ? But that took place at the latest in 4 B.C. ("Before Christ") or B.C.E. ("Before the Common Era"), if we are to accept the evidence of the Gospels that King Herod the Great of Judea (37-4 B.C.) was still alive when Jesus was born. Who is responsible for the miscalculation? Who thought up the idea of a Christian or Common Era anyway? And where did the idea originate?

It may come as a surprise to learn that the idea of a Christian Era dates back no further than the sixth century—A.D. It was a rather obscure Syrian monk named Dionysius Exiguus (Dennis the Little) who came up with it—and who miscalculated its "epoch" or starting point. His example was followed in the seventh century by the invention of a Moslem Era dating from the Hegira, the flight of Mohammed from Mecca to Medina in 622 A.D. Because the Moslem year is a lunar one and shorter than the solar year of the Christian calendar, as this book goes to press in 2002 A.D. the Moslem year has reached 1423 A.H. (*Anno Hegirae*), even though only 1,380 solar years have elapsed. In the eighth century A.D., the Jews followed suit with an era of their own based on the "year of creation," which according to tradition occurred in 3760 B.C. The Jewish year is a luni-solar one, based on the moon but reconciled periodically with the solar year by means of leap-months, so its years keep pace with the Christian calendar. In 2002 A.D., the Jewish year is calculated 3760 + 2002 = 5762.

Thus, early in the Middle Ages, the three great monotheistic faiths began dating their own eras, and these usages now dominate the globe. But they were far from the first to introduce the idea of the era as such. Like many of our most essential modern institutions, the concept of the era dates back before modern times, indeed before medieval and classical times, all the way to the ancient Near East, the best documented area of the world for half of its recorded history. The story unfolded in two stages.

The immediate model for the religious eras was the Seleucid Era, which was used in the Mediterranean world from before the rise of the Roman Empire to well after its fall. Its "epoch" was the (re-)conquest of Babylon by one of the successors of Alexander the Great, namely Seleucus I. In 312 B.C. Seleucus became the ruler of much of the Asian Near East, naming his son Antiochus I as co-regent late in his reign. Antiochus (and his descendants) continued to date by the years of Seleucus's reign even after the latter's death, and thus was born the novel idea of

This cuneiform tablet is the first in a series of clay tablets collectively known as the Babylonian Chronicle, which records major events beginning with the reign of the eighth-century B.C. Babylonian king Nabonassar.

the dynastic era. It replaced the cumbersome system of starting a new era with the accession of each new king, which required memorizing the lengths of previous reigns (or written king lists) to calculate long-term contracts or to write history. So useful was the new idea that it soon spread beyond the borders of the Seleucid kingdom. Thus the dynastic Seleucid Era became a truly international era, sometimes known as the "Era of (all) the Greeks" (see the First Book of Maccabees 1:10).

But even the Seleucid Era had its limitations. After its introduction, the development of astronomy proceeded apace, led by such figures as Hipparchus in the second century B.C. and Ptolemy in the second century A.D. They required a system that went back before Alexander, and Ptolemy in particular provided one in the form of the "Era of Nabonassar," named for the king who ascended the throne of Babylon in 747 B.C. According to Berossos, a Babylonian priest writing in Greek in the third century B.C., Nabonassar was responsible for introducing a new historiography in Babylon. The question is, did Nabonassar introduce the era named for him, or was it a construct of later historians and astronomers? The fact that two other eras, both devised in the third century B.C., dated their epochs to the eighth century B.C. supports the latter view. One of these was the Olympic Era, which was counted beginning with the first Olympiad in 776 B.C. The other was the Roman Era, dated "from the founding of Rome" (*ab urbe condita*), supposedly in 753 B.C.

But cuneiform records from Babylonia suggest otherwise. They show that numerous calendric reforms as well as innovations in chronological historiography, or what may be termed "chronography," do in fact go back to King Nabonassar. Among these are the so-called "Babylonian Chronicle," a year-by-year record of major events affecting Babylonia and especially its priesthood; semi-annual "diaries" with observations of astronomical, meteorological and other natural phenomena (together with fluctuations in commodity prices), and occasionally historical events; and the regularization of the system of "intercalation" of leap months—a system still largely adhered to by the Jewish calendar. So the possibility cannot be entirely ruled out that Nabonassar meant to introduce a new era beginning with his accession. True, political events frustrated his plans, for his son lost his throne to the Assyrians. But it is possible that astronomers continued to use the era, thus laying the groundwork for the later Seleucid Era and, ultimately, for our own era.

Signs of Life

Denise Schmandt-Besserat

Just 50 years ago, no one knew the origins of perhaps the greatest human invention of all time: writing. The clues lay in thousands of artifacts accumulating dust in the storerooms of the world's great museums. For 25 years, I visited museums in the Near East, Europe and North America, systematically examining clay objects from the Neolithic period (8000-6000 B.C.). Among figurines, spindle whorls, pots and mud-bricks, I found lots of minuscule clay tokens in many shapes. What were they? No one had any idea. I finally came to understand that these humble clay tokens were counters—and that they were the precursors of the earliest writing.

It all began about 7,500 B.C., when early farmers became concerned with keeping track of goods. They made counters out of clay in a dozen shapes, including cones, spheres, disks, cylinders, tetrahedrons and ovoids. Each shape was assigned a meaning. A cone, for example, stood for a small measure of grain, a sphere stood for a large measure of grain and a cylinder stood for an animal. The invention was simple but of the greatest

LOUVRE MUSEUM

DENISE SCHMANDT-BESSERAT/UNIVERSITY OF TEXAS AT AUSTIN

Over 5,000 years, from the mid-eighth millennium B.C. to the late third millennium B.C., writing evolved from simple signs denoting objects to a complex symbol-system capable of encoding human language. In the earliest stages, tokens of different shapes (lower photo) represented various goods in a one-to-one correspondence; one cone-shaped token, for example, represented one small measure of grain. In the middle of the fourth millennium B.C., tokens began to be placed in hollow clay envelopes, sometimes with the contents of the envelope impressed on its surface. The spherical envelope at top, from ancient Susa in present-day Iran, is impressed with seven markings representing the seven tokens it contained.

importance: It was the first visual code, the first symbol system ever created for the sole purpose of communicating.

There are about 8,000 of these tokens, from Palestine, Anatolia, Syria, Mesopotamia and Iran. Clearly such accounting practices were common throughout the Near East. Four millennia later, when cities first appeared, tokens rather suddenly evolved into a complex accounting system with a repertory of 300 shapes, some with incised or punched markings used to record multiple types of goods. There were tokens for keeping track of raw materials like wool and metal; processed foods like bread, honey and trussed ducks; and manufactured goods like textiles, mats and vessels.

This token system, while a brilliant initial step, was cumbersome. Tokens were used to represent goods in a one-to-one correspondence—one cone for one small measure of grain, ten ovoids for ten jars of oil. This meant, in effect, that these ancient Mesopotamians could keep track of only small amounts of goods.

Around 3500 B.C. the administrators of city-states in Mesopotamia, Syria and Iran began placing tokens in envelopes to keep accounting records orderly and tamper-proof. We have 150 such envelopes in the form of hollow clay balls filled with tokens.

Some of these envelopes' surfaces bear impressions of the tokens they contained. Impressions were made by stamping tokens onto the wet clay of the envelope. The markings allowed officials to know the type and number of tokens in an envelope without opening it. This was the first real step toward writing, for now three-dimensional symbols (tokens) were represented by two-dimensional signs (envelope markings).

A dramatic simplification of this system occurred around 3300-3200 B.C., as we know from 200 tablets in collections

T. CUYLER YOUNG/ROYAL ONTARIO MUSEUM

In the late fourth millennium B.C., Mesopotamians began to dispense with tokens in favor of a numeral system. Now inventories were incised on clay tablets, and objects were recorded with the use of numbers along with a sign denoting the object. The sign for a large measure of grain, the sphere, was used to refer to "10" and the sign for a small measure of grain, the cone, was used to refer to "1." The 3100 B.C. tablet above, from Godin Tepe in Iran, is inscribed with signs for 44 objects (four spheres and four cones, which in two dimensions appear as circles and triangles).

from Mesopotamia, Iran and Syria. Instead of filling envelopes with tokens, record-keepers began to make impressions of the tokens on flattened clay balls. Thus were created the world's first tablets, or texts written on flattened clay—dispensing entirely with the actual counters. Consequently, the markings no longer merely represented tokens; they were independent signs standing for grain, sheep, oil or woven rugs.

Thus it took no fewer than four inventions—tokens, envelopes, markings and tablets—and about 4,000 years to fully reduce three-dimensional tokens to written signs. The system itself, however, had remained largely unchanged. Like the tokens, the impressed signs represented goods in one-to-one correspondence. Three small measures of grain were still represented by three cone impressions.

Around 3100 B.C., accountants began using a pointed stylus to draw the tokens—relieving them of the task of actually pressing tokens onto the tablet. Moreover, 4,000 tablets from

Sumerian Uruk illustrate that incised signs were not used to stand for objects in one-to-one correspondence. Ten jars of oil were no longer represented by ten ovoids. Instead, the sign for a jar of oil (the ovoid) was preceded by numerals, or signs for abstract numbers ("abstract" in the sense that a certain sign—for example, "3"—can be used without regard to what is counted: three goats, three cities or three ideas).

No new signs were created to express abstract numbers. Instead, the old impressed signs for grain measures took on new meanings. The cone sign that formerly represented a small measure of grain came to mean "1," and the sphere sign that formerly represented a large measure of grain came to mean "10." Here was a marvelous economy of signs: 33 jars of oil were expressed by seven signs (10 + 10 + 10 + 1 + 1 + 1 and "oil")—rather than 33 signs.*

Equally important, as a result of the creation of numerals, the signs for goods and the signs for numbers could evolve in separate ways. Writing and counting generated different sign systems.

Those 4,000 tablets from Uruk show that toward the end of the fourth millennium B.C. the names of people who gave or received goods began to be listed in inventories. This means that signs were invented that stood for sounds—that is, the name of the person as spoken in the Sumerian language. These new signs,

> ## OddiFacts
>
> *Back in Egypt*
>
> The Great Pyramid at Giza, built by Pharaoh Khufu (2551-2528 B.C.), consists of 2,300,000 limestone and granite blocks, each weighing about 2.5 tons. Khufu's workers labored for 23 years on this project—meaning that they laid a stone, on average, every five minutes.

---

*The base-10 system, however, was not the only number system used in ancient Mesopotamia. Grain and bread, among other things, tended to be counted in groups of 60 (in a sexagesimal number system). Other groupings were also used.

or phonograms, were sketches of easily drawn things that stood for the sound of the word they evoked. A drawing of a man stood for the sound "lu" and a drawing of a mouth stood for the sound "ka," which were the words for "man" and "mouth" in Sumerian. The syllables or words composing an individual's name were written like a rebus. For example, the name Lucas could have been written with the two signs mentioned above, man-mouth or "lu-ka." With the invention of phonograms, writing became connected with the sounds of speech.

In 2800 B.C. writing still dealt exclusively with accounting. Texts listed merchandise received or dispensed by a state administration, stipulated land donations or compiled signs (in a kind of dictionary) for the benefit of scribes. But then an extraordinary development occurred about 2700-2600 B.C. at the court of the Sumerian kings of Ur. Royal scribes began writing on objects of gold, silver and lapis lazuli that were to be deposited in tombs. The inscriptions consisted of a personal name— "Meskalamdug"—wrought on a gold bowl, or a name plus a title—"Puabi, Queen"—on a lapis lazuli seal.

For the first time in history, the Ur scribes put writing to work for a function other than accounting. That new purpose was funerary. The Sumerians believed that the name of a deceased individual was to be spoken aloud at regular intervals to sustain him or her in the underworld. The writing of Meskalamdug's name on a gold bowl to be buried with him suggests that writing the sounds of a name was deemed equivalent to speaking the name aloud. So after 5,000 years of dreary accounting work, writing began to be put to the more dignified task of guaranteeing the survival of the dead.

This concern for the afterlife led to another development in the history of writing. About 2600 or 2500 B.C. statues of men in the attitude of prayer were inscribed with the name of a deceased individual followed by a plea for a long afterlife. These prayers addressed to gods used sentences with subjects, verbs and complements—so that the earliest writing modeled itself on speech by adopting the syntax of spoken language.

Now we have mature writing, the gateway to literature. About 2400 B.C., the Sumerian ruler Eanatum, king of the city-state of Lagash, was able to describe his victories in a lengthy text. By 2000 B.C., writing was used for historical, religious, legal, scholarly and literary texts.

The origin of writing is no longer a mystery. The objects long ignored in museum storage—8,000 tokens, 150 envelopes, 20 inscribed envelopes, 200 impressed tablets, 4,000 incised tablets, a dozen funerary gifts, 80 worshiper statues—snap together like pieces of a puzzle. The puzzle's picture, however, is quite different from what one might have anticipated. Who could have suspected that writing has its roots deep in prehistory—going back to the ninth millennium B.C.? And who would ever have guessed that writing derived from counting?

In any event, is it not fitting and proper that the invention of our most powerful form of self-expression was connected to our mortality?

First Glass

Samuel Kurinsky

In museum vitrines all over the world, we see beautiful objects labeled "Roman Glass." This is misleading, for it is unlikely that any ancient Roman became a glassmaker.

Nor were the Greeks more knowledgeable about the art of glassmaking.

In 426 B.C. the playwright Aristophanes reported the astonishment of Greek ambassadors to the Persian court who were served in bowls made of a strange translucent material for which they had no name. Yet the art of glassmaking was already 2,000 years old.

Glassmaking was born in ancient Mesopotamia as an amalgamation of two independent technologies, the invention of glazes and of reverberatory furnaces (which produce high temperatures by radiating heat from the furnace's roof). The Sumerians had discovered the formula for glazing, a process of vitrification in which a thin film of glass forms on another surface. But they could not produce glass in bulk, because their pottery furnaces could not sustain the necessary temperature of over 2,000 degrees. In the mountains of northern Mesopotamia, however, Aramite and Hurrian smiths invented such high-temperature furnaces to smelt iron. When northern Mesopotamia and Sumer were conquered by the Aramite Sargon I around the 24th century B.C., the two technologies married and the art of glassmaking was born.

Glassmaking was invented only once in human history. Its secrets traveled from Akkadia to Canaan, following the path of the biblical Abraham. For over 2,000 years, the art languished in the Near East until Levantine practitioners brought it to Europe following the Roman conquest.

Two Roman emperors identified the glassmakers of their times as Jews. In writing to his consul Servianus, Hadrian (117-138 A.D.) reported that the Jews of Alexandria were "blowers of glass." In 301 A.D. the emperor Diocletian issued an edict fixing the prices of goods throughout the empire. Only two classes of glassware were listed: *vitri Alexandrini* (which, as Hadrian had reported a century and a half earlier, were made by Jews) and *vitri Iudaici*. The name "Judea" had been

expunged by Hadrian in 137 A.D. following the Bar Kochba rebellion, but the term *vitri Iudaici* was so ingrained in the Roman vernacular that it persisted for centuries as a generic term for glassware. Indeed, there is an extraordinary linkage of Jews and glassmaking throughout the Roman Empire. In Anatolia, no examples of glassmaking predate the arrival of Jewish communities, but such examples do appear wherever Jews settled, such as at Apameia, Acmoneia and Synnada. For another example, glass cullet (shards of manufactured

Black-and-white photos simply cannot do justice to the luminous diatreta *ware above, which was made by cutting away layers of glass, or to the multi-colored murrhine bowl opposite, which was inlaid with scores of glass tesserae.*

THE CORNING MUSEUM OF GLASS

glass used to catalyze the glassmaking process) and other evidence of glassworking were recovered from a Jewish shop nestled against the wall of Sardis's late-fourth-century A.D. synagogue.

Wealthy Romans had a hankering for vessels made of precious stone from the Near East, which prompted Near Eastern glassworkers to produce glass replicas. The Palestinian Talmud describes how riotously colored glass can be created by rolling together molten glass of various hues. It also describes how cameo effects are obtained by sculpting out upper layers of glass, creating an image that appears against the background of the lower layer. *Diatreta* glass, also described in the Palestinian Talmud, was an even greater tour de force: Its top layer was undercut and separated from the lower layer, producing a cage-like effect. Eastern glassmakers also wrought murrhine vessels, made of glass tesserae,

OddiFacts

Eco-Friendly They Weren't

Scientists have traced Roman pollution as far afield as Greenland, where a 9,000-foot ice core has revealed traces of lead contamination. Much of the lead, dating from 150 B.C. to 50 A.D., came from Rio Tinto, a mine in western Spain. Romans used lead in plumbing, architecture and ship building—and, unaware of its poisonous effects, as a protective coating for drinking vessels and cookware. Some scholars believe lead poisoning contributed to the fall of the Roman Empire.

whose brilliant color outshone mosaics made of natural stones.

The Latin word for glass, *vitreum*, first appears in an oration by Cicero in 54 B.C. in reference to an import. When the emperor Augustus added Egypt to the empire a little more than 20 years later, he demanded glassware as part of his tribute. Glassmakers from Alexandria—a city where Jews constituted 40 percent of the population— founded furnaces on the coast between Cumae and Liternum in 14 A.D. and at Porta Cassena in Rome. Pliny the Elder (c. 24-79 A.D.) mentions that glassmakers from Syria (the Romans tended to call Jews "Syrians," "Orientals" and "Palestinians") settled in the region of Campania, near the Volturnus River (*Natural History* 36:194).

It was probably in the Trastevere (across the Tiber) quarter that the production of glassware got underway in Rome itself, along with such other sooty and malodorous "Jewish" industries as smithing, unguent manufacturing and leather tanning. Trastevere was a dreary slum with crooked streets, dingy workshops and Rome's oldest synagogue. With the influx of some 20,000 to 40,000 free Jews to Rome by 50 A.D., the city took on a decidedly eastern flavor.

According to the renowned glass historian Axel von Saldern, Jewish glassmakers followed the Roman legions into the heart of Europe. "Although Syria-Palestine remains the cradle of 'modern' glass-making and Alexandria continued to produce fine luxury ware, Naples, Rome and northern Italy, southeastern France, Cologne and other cities along the Rhine could also claim an efficient industry established mainly by Jewish glassmakers emigrated from Palestine in the 1st century."* To choose just one of many examples, the oldest Judaic settlement in Germany was in Trier, and the first glasshouses of the Rhineland were founded there.

With the Christianization of the empire and burgeoning hostility against Jews, the art of glassmaking suffered. The church father St. Jerome (348-420 A.D.) penned a bitter treatise on the humiliating hold "Semitic" artisans had on the Roman world with their unique skills. He complained that these artisans, mosaicists and sculptors were everywhere, and that glassmaking was one of the trades "by which the Semites [Jews] captured the Roman world."**

The church launched a campaign to convert or displace the "stiff-necked Orientals" from manual trades by placing artisans' guilds under the patronage of Christian saints. The production of glass and glassware, however, presented a problem. "In Cologne ... where the guilds succeeded in ultimately barring Jews from almost all industrial occupations, [Jews were] still allowed to become glaziers, probably because no other qualified personnel was available."†

---

*Axel von Saldern, *Glas von der Antike bis zum Jugenstil* (Mainz am Rhine: Philipp von Zabern, 1980), p. 19.

**St. Jerome, Commentary on Ezekiel in the *Patrologia Latina* 8.27.313, "Orbe, Romano Occupato."

†Saló W. Baron, in Nachum Gross, ed., *Economic History of the Jews* (Jerusalem: Keter House, 1975), p.40.

The vitric arts, however, continued to flourish in the Near East. When Jewish sages compiled the Midrash from the rabbinic through the medieval periods (c. 300-1100 A.D.), they likened God's blowing the breath of life into Adam to the art of the glassblower. Throughout the Upper and Lower Galilee and in Judea, men continued to blow soul into hot glass.

Let the Games Begin!

William W. Hallo

We human beings like to think of ourselves as wise, as *homo sapiens*. But we share two of our most common qualities with the beasts. We are often murderous, and hence have been described as *homo necans* in a disquisition on violence (in relation to Greek sacrificial rites and myths) published under that title by Walter Burkert. And we are irrepressibly playful, as documented in Jan Huizinga's *Homo Ludens*.

Evidence of this universal playfulness goes deep into the past. Surprisingly, some of its manifestations have stayed recognizably similar over the millennia, such as dice and board games.

It may seem odd that so specific a phenomenon as dice should have its origin in antiquity, and yet that is true not only of the concept but of the precise form. The earliest dice known date to the second half of the third millennium B.C.; they come from the Indus Valley culture, in present-day Pakistan, and from Mesopotamia in the Early Dynastic III period (c. 2500-2300 B.C.). These ancient specimens look very much like modern dice, and some of them have dots arranged in the modern way (with dots on opposite sides adding up to seven). The Mesopotamians continued to play with dice in the second and first millennia B.C.; a late example from Babylon is even made of glass. Further west, in Palestine and Egypt, various shapes were experimented with, but the "modern" cubical shape and dot arrangement is also attested, for example in dice recovered in excavations at Ashkelon.

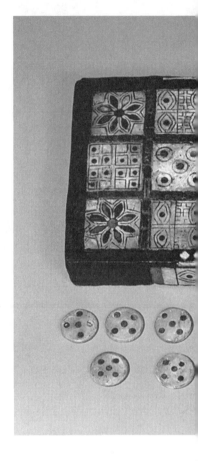

Some dice have been found in association with board games, which also have a hoary antiquity. The classic study of board games is a Latin treatise by the British orientalist Thomas Hyde (1636-1703), who also introduced the term *dactyli cuneiformes*, or cuneiform signs. Hyde's *De Ludis Orientalibus* was translated as *Chess: Its Origin* by Victor Keats (1995), who also gave us *Chess, Jews and History* (1994) and *Chess Among the Jews* (1995). But for all its fabled past in India or the Persian Near East, and its subsequent conquest of the world, chess is a relative newcomer on the scene. Checkers, too, which also uses a board of 64 squares, probably only goes back to Egyptian forerunners in the late second millennium B.C.

But there are far older board games, which come basically in three types.

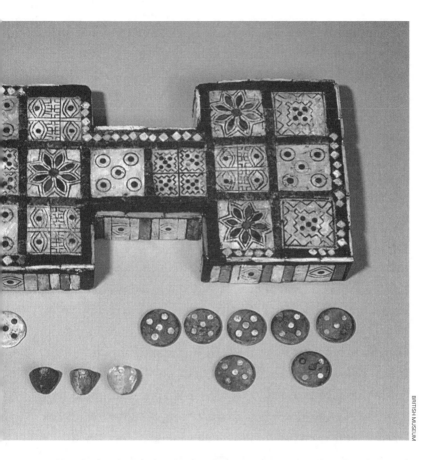

BRITISH MUSEUM

The rules for playing this third-millennium B.C. game, found in the Royal Cemetery at Ur and now housed in the British Museum, are unknown. The board is 10 inches long and 5 inches wide and consists of 20 squares inlaid with shell, lapis lazuli, red paste and red limestone. Two sets of seven counters and three pyramid-shaped dice were found with the board. Similar game boards are known from the eastern Mediterranean to India; each board is arranged with four rows of three squares connected to two rows of three squares by a bridge of two squares.

The simplest is a board with 58 holes arranged in four lines, with the two outside lines having 19 holes each and the two inside lines having 10 holes each. This game required counters to be moved from hole to hole according to certain rules. The counters, and the dice associated with the game, would have been pebbles or the knucklebones of sheep or other small animals (sometimes called astragali, from the Greek word *astragaloi*). The game board itself, though sometimes made of wood, ivory or even stone, was typically made of clay. This game has been played all over the Near East, from ancient times down to the present day.

A more sophisticated game board was found in the excavations of the Royal Graves at Ur, dating to the middle of the third millennium B.C. Elaborately carved and inlaid with shell and lapis lazuli, the board has 20 squares in seven different patterns. Variations on these 20-square game boards have been found at ancient Assyrian sites, in modern Lebanon (Kumidi), in the Indus Valley and at Shahr-I-Sokhta in northeastern Iran, the last in the form of a snake. This snake-shaped board from Iran suggests a connection with the *senet* game of Egypt, which has 20 to 30 squares typically arranged in the shape of a snake.

The most complicated ancient game board is represented by only two Mesopotamian examples. This board is divided into 84 fields by horizontal, vertical and diagonal lines. The inscription on one of the boards is probably the name of the game: *illat kalbē*, meaning "pack of dogs." The other board is inscribed more elaborately, not only with its date (177/176 B.C.) but also with its rules! According to Irving Finkel, who organized a colloquium on ancient board games for the British Museum, the rules call for two players to use five pieces named after birds and a die made from knucklebone. Finkel also discovered a survival of this game among the Jews of Cochin in southern India, where the game is played only by women and only on the Ninth of Ab—which is the Jewish fast day commemorating the destruction of the Temple.

That playfulness is a universal trait is not surprising. What is impressive, however, is that devices created to satisfy this craving have survived in similar form over such an extraordinarily long period of time and across so much of the world.

Inventing Time

Jack Meinhardt

If someone tells you that the Galápagos Islands, in the Pacific Ocean far off the coast of Ecuador, lie almost directly *south* of Chicago, you would probably consult one of the commonest objects of daily life, a map. The science of mapmaking, indeed, has its origins in ancient times—as Harold Brodsky observes in "Ptolemy Charts the World" on page 69.

Now, if you learned that Rio de Janeiro, Brazil, unexpectedly, is a couple of time zones ahead of New York, you might start thinking about time—and you might wonder about one of its basic units, the hour. Why are there 24 hours in a day, rather than 10, given that we use a decimal system? Stranger yet, why 60 minutes, and why 60 seconds?

It is perfectly possible to divide the day into 10 hours (or 100, or any number that is convenient) and the hour into 10 minutes (or 100). Over the millennia and around the globe, time has indeed been parceled out in different ways. As late as the fourth century A.D., the Romans divided daylight hours into only two parts—before midday (*ante meridiem*, or a.m.) and after midday (*post meridiem*, or p.m.)—though they later added designations for early morning, forenoon, afternoon and evening. Until the 19th century, the Japanese counted only six daylight "hours."

Our stern taskmistress Nature has determined some of the ways in which we reckon time: The year is governed by the Earth's revolution around the sun (some calendars, like the Jewish calendar, rely on lunar cycles, but these calendars generally have mechanisms that reorient them to the solar year) and the day by the Earth's rotation. But Nature is silent concerning the hour. The 24-hour day and the 60-minute hour are mere conventions, human inventions, quirks of history. This messy system for counting time, ultimately, should be blamed on the ancient Egyptians and Babylonians.

As early as 1300 B.C., the Egyptians were dividing the day into two parts: 12 equal daylight hours (sunrise to sunset) and 12 equal nighttime hours (sunset to sunrise). The Egyptians had apparently borrowed this system, along with much of their mathematics, from the Mesopotamians—pushing the origins of the hour even further back in time.

Why the number 12? The ancient Babylonians counted in units of 60 (whereas we count by tens); this is called a sexagesimal number system. So perhaps the Egyptians (or the Babylonians) divided the perfect number 60 by the number of then-known planets—Mercury, Venus, Mars, Jupiter and Saturn—producing the number 12. In any event, 12 was convenient as a factor of 60.

But this is not the hour we know, with its 24 regular 60-minute intervals pulsing around the clock. Rather, it is a variable, or seasonal, hour: Each of the 12 daylight hours is longer in the summer (when days are long) than in the winter; the duration of the seasonal hour also changes as one moves north or south. Daylight and nighttime hours are equal in length only twice a year, on the vernal and autumnal equinoxes. This variable division of the day suited the timekeeping tools available to the ancients: the sundial and gnomon (the Greek name for the vertical pole that casts a shadow on a dial), which pointed out hours not in regular intervals but according to the time of year and geographical location. Sundials are attested in late-second-millennium B.C. Egypt; literary evidence suggests that they were used during the early second millennium B.C. in Mesopotamia.*

The creation of the standardized hour, what scholars call the equinoctial hour, came later—perhaps as a result of a new kind of technology, the water clock (called by the Greeks a *clepsydra*, literally meaning "water thief"). Water clocks measure time in absolute, rather than variable, intervals; they were used, for instance, to keep orators from speaking too long in Athenian law courts.

Exactly when the day was divided into 24 equal hours remains under debate: It may have coincided with the creation of Hellenistic astronomical schools, or it may have come much later, around the 13th century A.D. Whether a Greek or medieval invention, it was based on the 24-hour day used by ancient Egyptians and Babylonians.

Perhaps in the 13th century, with the invention of accurate mechanical clocks, the hour was subdivided into minutes (from the Latin *pars minuta prima*, or "first small part") and seconds (*partes minutae secundae*).

*This chapter is deeply indebted to William W. Hallo's *Origins: The Ancient Near Eastern Background of Some Modern Western Institutions* (Brill, 1996).

Although this development moves us out of the ancient world, we should note that it, too, was a tribute to the old Babylonian sexagesimal system. Medieval chronologists divided the hour into 60 minutes and 60 seconds, following Ptolemy's division of each degree of a circle into 60 minutes, with each minute containing 60 seconds. (The convention of dividing the circle into 360 degrees, still in use today, was probably invented by the ancient Egyptians, who again made use of the Babylonian sexagesimal system. The small superscripted circle we use to designate degrees, as in the 360° of a circle, probably derives from an Egyptian hieroglyphic, perhaps representing the sun, meaning "day.")

Whether you knew it or not, as the second hand of your watch moves steadily around the minute, and as the minute hand moves around the hour, you are counting as the Babylonians did, by 60s.

The Horoscope Casters

Alexander Jones

For the Greeks and Romans of the first century B.C., the term "Chaldean" had two meanings: It was the name of the inhabitants of Chaldea, a district of southern Babylonia, and it was the title given to professional diviners who used the heavens to predict the future. This second group got its name from the popular belief that horoscope casting was invented in ancient Mesopotamia.

Although traditions of divination often appeal to ancient authorities for credibility, the Chaldean origins of astrology are no fiction. Since the 1880s, about 30 ancient Babylonian cuneiform tablets containing horoscopes have surfaced. The majority of these texts were first made accessible for study in Francesca Rochberg's excellent 1998 volume, *Babylonian Horoscopes*. Thanks to this publication, we now know that the horoscope was one of the last and—for better or worse—one of the most enduring contributions of ancient Mesopotamia to human culture.

The origins of Babylonian astrology can be traced back to the Old Babylonian period (early second millennium B.C.), when royal diviners began interpreting the significance of celestial

"The son of Tar-sa-mu-ku-us, born on September 1, 288 B.C. [or the ancient equivalent thereof]" reads the cuneiform inscription on this 2-inch-wide Babylonian horoscope tablet, now in the British Museum. Ancient astrologers, much like their modern counterparts, cast horoscopes by connecting a person's birth date to certain astronomical facts, such as the positions of the moon, sun and planets. This inscription refers to an autumnal equinox and total lunar eclipse that had occurred not long before Tar-sa-mu-ku-us was born.

BRITISH MUSEUM

omens, such as eclipses. But after the Persians conquered Mesopotamia in the mid-first millennium B.C., Babylonian astrologers started using the heavens to predict ordinary people's fates.

There was nothing new in the idea of using a person's birth date to foretell his future: A seventh-century B.C. omen series called *Iqqur īpuš* used the month of birth for just this purpose. There was a technical obstacle, however, to bringing the heavens into play. How could ancient diviners do this when there was no assurance that an ominous occurrence could be seen on a particular person's birth date—for example, on rainy or cloudy days? The Babylonians solved this problem by taking into account a combination of astronomical events that occurred before and after the target date, along with certain facts about the situation of the heavenly bodies on that date.

> ## OddiFacts
>
> ### Going My Way?
>
> Two thousand years before Heaven's Gate cult members strapped themselves in for a journey into eternity aboard the starship Hale-Bopp, Julius Caesar hitched a similar ride. In 44 B.C., just after Caesar's murder, a comet loomed in the Roman skies—so bright it could be seen for a week in broad daylight. The Romans believed this celestial visitor was a sign of Caesar's deification. Thus Augustus, whom Caesar had adopted in 45 B.C., proclaimed himself "Son of God" when he became the first Roman emperor in 27 B.C.

Where did their astronomical data come from? In *Against the Professors*, the second-century A.D. Greek philosopher Sextus Empiricus offers us the fanciful picture of a Chaldean watching the sky, awaiting the sound of a gong signaling that a child has been born. In reality, horoscopes were prepared well after the moment of birth, and there was no call for such precise timing. Astrologers could turn to the archive at the Esagila Temple of

Marduk, for instance, where Babylonian scientists had been keeping a continuous record of astronomical and meteorological observations since at least the seventh century B.C. Their so-called Astronomical Diaries seem to have been the source of much of the information in ancient Babylonian horoscopes.*

All the Babylonian horoscope tablets, with a single early exception, employ zodiacal signs to specify the locations of the sun, moon and planets (Mercury, Venus, Mars, Jupiter and Saturn) on a person's date of birth. It had long been recognized that the moon and planets travel along a fixed belt among the stars, and that their positions could be expressed either in relation to certain bright stars in this so-called Path of the Moon or, more roughly, according to the constellation through which they were passing. The zodiacal signs used in Babylonian horoscopes represented 12 equal divisions of this belt, and they were named for the constellations that more or less coincided with those divisions.

Thus the constellations called the Hired Man, the Bull of Heaven, the Great Twins, and the Crab gave their names to zodiacal signs corresponding to our Aries, Taurus, Gemini and Cancer. To determine when a planet crossed from one zodiacal sign to the next, the observers of the Astronomical Diaries tracked its passage through the stars; for example, the star called the Rear Twin (our Eta Geminorum or Pollux) marked the boundary between the Great Twins and the Crab. Each zodiacal sign was, in turn, comprised of 30 smaller units, called *ki* (our degrees), which could be used to pinpoint the location of heavenly bodies more precisely.

*A handful of horoscopes from Uruk suggest that a different routine may have been followed there, drawing not on records of observation but on calculations based on mathematical theories of the motions of heavenly bodies.

Most of the Babylonian horoscope tablets that have survived contain only the date of birth of a person and the relevant astronomical data. Only a few tablets—mostly from Uruk—actually offer any kind of prophecy or interpretation: "His days will be long" or "He will have sons" are typical predictions. These notes seem to have been derived mechanically by looking up a particular astronomical fact, say the moon's position, in an omen list. One must presume that the horoscope caster who inscribed the tablet also regaled his customer with stories that wove together, embellished and, if necessary, reconciled inconsistencies between these omens.

The Babylonian horoscope casters apparently left no literature or correspondence explaining how a horoscope worked. We cannot say whether they, like their omen-watching predecessors, believed that the heavens expressed the personal intentions of the gods—though horoscopes dealt with periodic and predictable astronomical phenomena, properties not usually associated with divine whims.

When the Greeks first began studying Babylonian horoscopy, in the first or second century B.C., they had no trouble interpreting the horoscope as a record of physical cause-and-effect relationships. The heavenly bodies, revolving in complex orbits around the earth, were seen as agents of nature; their motions helped determine the interaction of elements on earth, including the birth and growth of human infants.

About 200 Greek horoscopes survive from antiquity, mostly in the form of papyri from Egypt. The earliest ones date from the late first century B.C., just a few decades after the last known Babylonian horoscope.

Horoscopic astrology burst forth on the classical world at an opportune moment. Methods of divination and magic were rapidly gaining popularity at the same time that theoretical astronomy was steadily advancing. By building on principles laid out by the Babylonians, Greek astrologers could claim to satisfy practical human needs through modern, scientifically respectable methods. Like their Babylonian predecessors, ancient Greek horoscopes eschew interpretation, normally giving no more than the date and time of birth and a list of astronomical facts. They focus tightly on the hour of birth, disregarding eclipses and other possibly divine omens that take place well before or well after a person's birth.

There are some striking differences between ancient Greek and ancient Babylonian horoscopes. Greek horoscopes list not only the basic zodiacal positions of the sun, the moon and the five planets; they also record the *horoskopos* or "hour-watcher"— the part of the zodiac that was rising on the eastern horizon at the moment of a person's birth. This element, which was not included by the Babylonians, is what gave the horoscope its name. In addition, all of the astronomy in the Greek horoscope was computed by means of tables; observations of the heavens played no direct role in Greco-Roman astrology.

Extant ancient Greek astrology textbooks reveal that Greek horoscope interpretations involved a much higher degree of mathematical sophistication than anything in Mesopotamian divination. Nevertheless, the intellectual heritage of astrology is clear. Despite numerous changes and innovations over the centuries, modern horoscopy would still be perfectly intelligible to a Greek of the time of the Antonines (the second century A.D.), and it would not be wholly foreign to a Babylonian of the time of Alexander the Great.

3.14159265...

Kim Jonas

How do you find the holy grail of mathematics?
You start with a circle, which is the easiest geometric shape to draw (just fix one end of a string in place and swing the other end around it). Then measure the circle's perimeter (also known as the circumference) and the distance across its widest point (the diameter). Divide the circumference by the diameter—and you have that well-known but eternally daunting number π, or *pi*, which has a value of 3.14159265...

That is part of the mystique of π: Whatever the size of the circle, the value remains the same (it's what mathematicians call a "constant"). Unfortunately, π is also "irrational," meaning that it is impossible to calculate its value completely; the decimals go on forever without regular repetition.

Calculating the value of π has been a puzzle for millennia. One of the earliest implied values is given in a biblical passage describing the construction of a huge basin for Solomon's Temple: "Then [Hiram of Tyre] made the molten sea; it was round, ten cubits from brim to brim, and five cubits high. A line

OddiFacts

Arab-ish

The flowering of science and mathematics in the medieval Islamic world had a great impact on the English language. Many mathematical terms we use today were borrowed from Arabic: algebra (*al-Jabr*), algorithm (*al-Khawarizmî*), zenith (*cenit*), azimuth (*al-sumut*) and cipher (*sifr*). Our medical vocabulary owes a similar debt to the Arabic scholarship that entered Europe mainly through Spain and Sicily: elixir (*al-Aksir*), alcohol (*al-kohl*), alchemy (*al-kimiya*), camphor (*kafur*) and aorta (*avarta*).

of thirty cubits would encircle it completely" (I Kings 7:23). In other words, $\pi = 30 \div 10$, or 3.

The Temple craftsmen obviously obtained these numbers through direct measurement—perhaps using a rope—and they came up with a simple approximation of π. More than a thousand years earlier, the Sumerians had developed a mathematical method for measuring a circle's dimensions by inscribing equilateral polygons (a geometric shape with three or more straight sides) inside the circle. The ancient Sumerians realized that the perimeter of a polygon inscribed in a circle would always be slightly smaller than the circle's circumference. This allowed them to make a fairly accurate measurement of a curved line, which is almost impossible to do with ordinary measuring devices.

According to a 4,000-year-old cuneiform tablet discovered in 1936, the Sumerians found that the ratio of the perimeter of a hexagon to the perimeter of the circle in which it is inscribed is $^{3456}\!/_{3600}$, which factors out to $^{216}\!/_{225}$. The Sumerians could thus measure any circle simply by measuring an inscribed polygon and making the adjustment. Then they could measure the circle's diameter—a simple straight line—and divide it into the circumference, producing an approximation of π. In this way, the Sumerians found π to be $3\ ^{23}\!/_{216}$ (3.1065), a much better calculation of π than the biblical value. Why wasn't this known to the Israelites at the time of Solomon? We'll never know.

In an ancient Egyptian mathematical treatise known as the Rhind Papyrus (c. 1650 B.C.), a scribe named Ahmes states that a certain circular field 9 units across (that is, with a diameter of 9) had an area of 64 units. Today, we know the relationship between the diameter, circumference and area of a circle: Area equals π multiplied by the square of the radius (half the diameter), or a = πr^2. Changing this equation around, we find that π equals the area divided by the square of the radius. The field's radius is 4.5 (half of nine); the square of 4.5 is 20.25; and 64 divided by 20.25 equals 3.16. Therefore, π = 3.16. Thus some modern commentators have given Ahmes credit for a close approximation of π. But was our ancient Egyptian scribe aware of this formula? Almost certainly not. He didn't know he was approximating π, and I should not like to give him credit for it.

Our next significant player is the Greek philosopher Antiphon. In the late fifth century B.C., he realized that if successive polygons were inscribed within a circle, doubling the number of sides each time, the difference between the polygon's perimeter and the circle's circumference would diminish toward zero (think of a circle as a polygon with an infinite number of sides). While Antiphon didn't calculate π using his method (as far as we know), his idea would be the basis of all improvements in the value of π until the 17th century A.D.

Two centuries after Antiphon, Archimedes (c. 287-212 B.C.) inscribed a hexagon in a circle, and then he kept doubling the number of sides until he had a 96-sided polygon inscribed in the circle. At the same time, he superscribed a similar series of polygons outside the circle. By this method, he found that π was greater than 3.14084 and less than 3.14286—an extremely close approximation of the actual value (3.14159265). Archimedes was the first mathematician to bound π in this way, by calculating its upper and lower limits. Thus he should be credited with making the search for the value of π a science.

For almost 2,000 years, no one improved on Archimedes's method of inscribed and superscribed polygons, though refinements were made in the calculation. The second-century A.D. Alexandrian astronomer Ptolemy, for instance, used Archimedes's method to reach a value of 3.14167. And the method was invented independently by Indian and Chinese mathematicians. In the fifth century A.D., the Chinese mathematician Tsu Chung-Chih and his son Tsu Keng-Chih, using the polygon method, found that π falls between 3.1415926 and 3.1415927, which is precise enough for most purposes even today.

The calculation of accurate trigonometric tables in the 16th century made the Archimedian approach much easier to pursue than before. The French lawyer and amateur mathematician François Viète (1540-1603) used trigonometry to calculate the perimeter of a polygon with 393,216 sides, pinpointing π somewhere between 3.1415926535 and 3.1415926537.

But it was Isaac Newton's development of calculus that reduced the calculation of π to plain old arithmetic. In 1655, the mathematician John Wallis published his proof of the infinite product $\pi \div 2 = 2 \times \frac{2}{3} \times \frac{4}{3} \times \frac{4}{5} \times \frac{6}{5} \times \frac{6}{7} \ldots$ And James Gregory, in 1671, found the infinite sum of $\pi \div 4 = 1 - \frac{1}{3} + \frac{1}{5} - \frac{1}{7} + \frac{1}{9} - \frac{1}{11} \ldots$ These formulas take hundreds of steps to arrive at even the first few digits of π, but they demonstrated the feasibility of the new method. Within a few years, Newton found a series of formulas that quickly gave him a 16-digit expansion of π. From then on, further computation of π was only a matter of desire and endurance.

When it comes to endurance, nothing can beat a computer. In 1949, the primitive ENIAC computer, the first of the "giant brains," was fed an algorithm for calculating π. Three days later, it arrived at an answer 2,037 digits long. Today programs are available that allow you to calculate a billion digits of π on your home computer over the weekend.

What's the point of computing π out that far? There is none. If we knew the diameter of the universe, the first 30 digits of π would theoretically enable us to calculate its circumference to within a millimeter. That's closer than we would ever need to come; the rest is just showing off.

Interesting Developments

Michael Hudson

It's hard enough for economists to explain whether interest rates will go up or down in today's world. How can we possibly hope to understand how the practice of charging interest began in the first place? When did people begin issuing interest-bearing loans? And how did they decide how much to charge for the privilege of borrowing money?

The answer to these questions turns out to be quite simple, once one understands how ancient Sumer, Babylonia, Greece and Rome set their interest rates. Indeed, simplicity of calculation was what these ancient economies strove for above all else.

Unlike today, interest rates in the ancient world did not rise and fall. Instead each society had its own steady or "normal" interest rate. This rate was often fixed by law—Hammurabi's code and Roman law both codified interest rates—though surviving contracts show an array of variations around the norm. Sumerian text exercises, used to train scribes, confirm the prevalence of these normal interest rates.

*This 7-foot-high stela from Susa depicts the Babylonian king
Hammurabi (1792-1750 B.C.) appealing to the enthroned god
Shamash. Its base is inscribed with Hammurabi's law code, which
standardized interest rates. Hammurabi also sought to control the
mounting burden of interest payments by issuing four "clean slate"
proclamations that canceled debts.*

How did this customary rate of interest come to be charged? And how did the rate manage to remain so steady, decade after decade and century after century? The rates could not have been set by market forces of supply and demand, for economic conditions must have changed every year and even seasonally.

A quick review of a few ancient civilizations' interest rates reveals that a strong non-economic factor was at work. Starting around 2000 B.C. in Mesopotamia, the normal commercial rate of interest was equivalent to 20 percent per year. I say "equivalent to" because the Sumerian interest rate was not expressed as a percentage. Ancient societies did not use percentages; instead, they relied on systems of fractions. The Sumerians, for example, used a sexagesimal (base-60) system to calculate fractions—a system that was later borrowed to divide the hour into 60 minutes, the minute into 60 seconds, and the circle into 360 degrees. They thus divided the ancient mina (their basic unit of currency) into 60 shekels. Like the fraction $\frac{1}{10}$ in our own decimal system, the shekel was the "unit fraction" of Sumerian mathematics.

This sexagesimal fraction system made it easy for the Mesopotamians to compute interest rates: Creditors simply charged all debtors $\frac{1}{60}$ of the principal amount per month. Over the course of a year, this worked out to an annual interest rate of 12 shekels per mina or $\frac{12}{60}$ of the principal amount (20 percent in our own decimal system).

In ancient Greece, the normal interest rate was fixed at ten percent. This rate was no doubt tied to the common Greek fractional unit, the *dekate* ($\frac{1}{10}$). The *dekate* was a standard unit of measurement for many economic transactions—for instance, the Greek military traditionally donated one *dekate* (or $\frac{1}{10}$) of its booty to the temples.

Public Works

In about 497 B.C., a quarter century after the Persians conquered Egypt, the Persian king Darius built the first Suez Canal. Completing a project begun by the Egyptian pharaoh Necho II (610-595 B.C.), Darius cut a 53-mile-long canal from Tell el-Maskuta, in the eastern Nile Delta, to the Gulf of Suez. To commemorate this engineering achievement, Darius laid down a series of stelae—at least three of which have been recovered—showing us the course of the ancient waterway.

The Romans used the duodecimal system, based on the fractional unit $\frac{1}{12}$ (a system probably derived from the number of months in the Julian calendar). For centuries, their interest rate was fixed by law at $\frac{1}{12}$ of the principal. In our base-10 decimal system this interest rate would be expressed rather cumbersomely as $8\frac{1}{3}$ percent (0.08333333). But in Rome's numerical system it worked out neatly to one "ounce" of interest per "pound" of credit. (The value of Roman currency was determined by its weight. The basic unit of measurement was the *libra*, or pound, which weighed about $\frac{3}{4}$ of one of our English pounds and was divided into 12 *unciae* or ounces.)

These examples clearly illustrate that ancient economies simply fixed their interest rates in the way that made them easiest to calculate: The local numbering system's basic unit-fraction—$\frac{1}{60}$, $\frac{1}{10}$ or $\frac{1}{12}$—was adopted as the normal rate of interest.

This method of determining interest rates seems to have persisted through the Byzantine era. Initially, the Byzantine empire's 12 percent interest rate worked out to a simple payment of one *nomisma* (or Byzantine penny, and the source of our "numismatics") per month. But after the reign of Constantine, the imperial currency was devalued, reducing the number of *nomismata* from 100 to 72 per pound of gold. The Byzantine interest rate was also adjusted accordingly, climbing from $\frac{1}{100}$ of the principal amount to $\frac{1}{2}$.

For many years, economists were baffled by the long-term fluctuations in ancient civilizations' interest rates. Clearly, the normal annual interest rate declined over time from Mesopotamia's 20 percent to Greece's 10 percent to Rome's 8⅓ percent. But why?

The discovery of this pattern led some economists to imagine that there was some innate law of civilization by which the rate of interest tended to decline. With our modern ways of thinking, it is easy to imagine that interest rates were being set according to a borrower's expected earnings or some other rational economic factor.

According to this explanation, loan profits and productivity rates fell as a result of population growth and technological innovation. Certainly, an investor's degree of financial risk seems to have diminished with the progress of civilization. In more advanced, relatively stable economies, creditors no longer had to protect themselves by charging the exorbitant interest rates of the distant past.

These sophisticated economic theories fail to take into account the simple fact that ancient interest rates were rooted in the local system of weights and measures. Clearly, interest rates in the ancient world declined over the millennia not because of any complex economic transformations, but rather because of simple changes in the systems of arithmetic and fractions being used.

The very fact that ancient civilizations set their interest rates in this non-economic way may help to explain why chronic debt plagued so many ancient cultures. Driven by abject need, agrarian debtors in ancient Babylon, Judea and Israel were often forced to borrow money at much higher rates of interest than they could possibly afford to pay. With interest rates regularly exceeding profit and crop-surplus rates, these societies inevitably experienced widespread economic polarization and financial instability. The problem of debt arrears (including unpaid taxes) was so common in Mesopotamia that the royal government periodically had to step in and regulate the economy. Between 2400 and 1700 B.C., the government issued the royal *amargi*, *andurarum* and *misharum* "clean slate" proclamations, canceling all non-trade-related agrarian debts—in part, no doubt, as a means of restoring balance to an economy plagued by overly high interest rates. Today's credit card holders with large balances may well long for a similar reprieve.

You Can Look It Up!

J. Harold Ellens

When I ask my ten-year-old grandson to bike over to the college library down the street and fetch me a book, I am always surprised how quickly he returns. He just punches a few buttons on the library computer, selects an author or title, and right there in front of him, displayed on the monitor, is the location of the book in the library. Half a million books and he gets the right one in seconds, at ten years of age.

When I was ten (many years ago), there was no such thing as a computer. But even then I could go to the town library for my father and, in half an hour or so, find the right book. Inside the front door of our Greco-Roman-looking library was a neat cabinet with lots of little drawers—the card catalogue. All the authors and titles of the library's books were arranged in alphabetical order, telling how the books were organized on the shelves. There were the sections for literature, history, arts, social sciences, natural sciences and religion. It worked like the computer does for my grandson, though it took me a little longer and I did not have such a nice skinny-tired "racer" to ride home.

People have been working imaginatively for 5,000 years to keep track of, store, and retrieve information they want to remember. Archaeologists digging in Mesopotamia tell us that before 3000 B.C. people were keeping track of things they were buying and selling, and of money others owed them, by making marks on clay tablets. Before that they probably made notches on sticks or stones to remember things.

When writing became popular and books or scrolls began to appear in great numbers, the problem became more complicated. So a man named Callimachus of Cyrene (c. 305-235 B.C.) developed the world's first card catalogue to organize the books (scrolls) in the immense collection of the ancient library of Alexandria in Egypt.

The Alexandria Library was established by Ptolemy I Soter in 306 B.C., some 25 years after Alexander the Great had founded the city in the Nile Delta. By the time of Jesus, the library held a million volumes. Here, around 300 B.C., Euclid wrote his study of plane geometry, *Elements*; here Eratosthenes of Cyrene (c. 275-195 B.C.) accurately measured the Earth's circumference. The library contained books from Mesopotamia, Anatolia, the Levant, Greece and North Africa. Here the works of the great classical authors, like Homer and Plato, were first redacted.

Callimachus apparently began working at the library after he turned 20. By the mid-third century B.C., the library's collection grew to more than 500,000 volumes. To keep track of all these books, Callimachus created a library catalogue called the Pinakes—which worked just as well as your Pentium, though it took a little longer.

Although the Pinakes has disappeared, we know a lot about it because ancient authors referred to it. (Perhaps the current excavations at the site of the library will find a copy.) In the tenth century A.D., for example, the great Arab scientist Ibn al-Nadim, a professor at the university in Baghdad, published the *Fihrist*, a survey of all the literature known in Islamic culture at that time; al-Nadim organized his work on the model of Callimachus's Pinakes.

The ancient Greek word *pinakes* literally means "tablets" or "tiles." Originally, *pinakes* probably referred to ceramic tiles that were fixed to the end of the library's scroll bins, identifying the nature of the works contained in each bin. Before Callimachus developed his card catalogue, such tiles were probably used to keep track of whole classes of scrolls in the library's various bins. Modern libraries use a similar system to identify books in stacks. Callimachus likely expanded on this tile system in organizing and recording the Alexandria Library collection. Callimachus's ancient catalogue consisted of 120 scrolls, in which all the Alexandria Library books (scrolls) were organized by discipline. Its subtitle was *The Tablets of the Outstanding Works in the Whole of Greek Civilization*.

The subject categories in the library included the humanities, the natural sciences and the social sciences. These subjects

OddiFacts

Out with the Old ...

Ever since Callimachus of Cyrene invented the first card catalogue in the third century B.C. for the library at Alexandria, libraries have arranged books according to subject matter. But that may soon change. The Library of Congress—home to more than 113,000,000 volumes—announced that it is considering a new space-saving system. To accommodate the 5,000 items received each day, the library plans to shelve books according to size rather than subject matter. The location of each book will be stored in a computer. This system will conserve shelf space, but critics fear that it will also eliminate opportunities for browsing. No wonder Callimachus said, "A big book is a big evil."

were further divided into epic poetry, nondramatic poetry, drama and miscellaneous literature; history, philosophy, oratory and law; and mathematics, medicine and other natural sciences.*

A great deal of bibliographical detail was also given for each book. The Pinakes identified each volume by its title and then recorded the name and birthplace of the author, the name of the author's father and teachers, the place and nature of the author's education, any nickname or pseudonym applied to the author, a short biography including a list of the author's works, a comment on their authenticity (that is, whether the works were really written by the author), the first line of the work specified, a brief digest of the volume, the source from which the book was acquired (such as the city where it was bought or the ship from which it was confiscated), the name of the former owner, the name of the scholar who redacted the text, and the total number of lines in each work. An immense task for over half a million books!

Thus Callimachus has been called the "Father of Bibliography." He helped fix forever the ways in which books and ideas would be catalogued—as in, say, our Library of Congress. We have simply borrowed Callimachus's idea and built upon it.

If you pick up the *Encyclopædia Britannica* and crack it open, you will quickly sense a correspondence between the way an encyclopedia is organized and the way your library is catalogued. Books and encyclopedia entries are organized alphabetically by subject, and each subject is a large rubric, drawing under a single heading masses of information that might have been organized differently.

---

*For more information, see Mostafa El-Abbadi, *Life and Fate of the Ancient Library of Alexandria* (Paris: UNESCO/UNDP, 1990).

This organization of *all* learning is called the Encyclopedia of Knowledge, which refers not to a set of books but to relationships we perceive among various kinds of information and ideas. We've determined that Herodotus's histories are more closely related to Homer's epics than to Euclid's geometry—and that geometry is closely related to astronomy and (much later) chemistry. We have organized our libraries, encyclopedias and university departments with this in mind. So firmly are these relationships embedded in our thinking that we forget the system had to be invented.

That's what Callimachus did in Alexandria.

Ptolemy Charts the World

Harold Brodsky

North is usually located at the top of a map. But this is simply a convention, determined by a historical twist of fate. Medieval European mapmakers generally placed east at the top, possibly to *orient* their maps toward the rising sun. Islamic maps of the Middle Ages, on the other hand, generally show south as up, placing the sacred city of Mecca proudly near the top of the world.

We prefer a northerly orientation, just as we prefer to read English from left to right—*tfel ot thgir naht rehtar*. But Arabic and Hebrew are read from right to left, Chinese is read down a column, and these directions work just as well. Maps with south, east or west at the top would do just fine, if we could get used to it.

The convention of making maps with north up top probably comes from the great Alexandrian geographer Ptolemy (c. 90-168 A.D.). When Ptolemy's *Hyphegesis Geographike* (*Guide to Geography*) became widely known in the 15th century, mapmakers followed his lead by placing north at the top. Since the world Ptolemy knew was about twice as wide (east-west) as high (north-

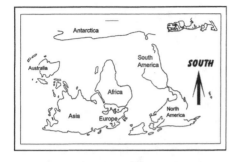

south), it was convenient to view it on a wide rectangular sheet. And the earliest maps based on Ptolemy's records were drawn on parchment, which is easier to unroll sideways. Ptolemy also suggested that the north-south position of a place could be calculated by measuring the angle between the horizon and the North Star. Therefore, all maps using Ptolemy's coordinates give special importance to north.

Unfortunately, Ptolemy's second-century A.D. *Geography* was lost to European civilization for more than a millennium. Toward the end of the 14th century, a copy of the work in a Greek codex (a manuscript bound into a book with leaves, rather than rolled up like a scroll) was found in Constantinople and brought to Florence; a Latin translation was completed in 1406. The modern science of cartography began with this reintroduction of Ptolemy's *Geography* to Western civilization.

Ptolemy knew that the sky held the key to accurate mapping. He was not the first to realize this; ancient travelers had long reached their destinations by making observations of the sun and stars. Nor was Ptolemy the first to suggest that the heavens be used to make world maps. More than 200 years before Ptolemy the Greek astronomer Hipparchus (c. 190-126 B.C.), who developed an accurate method for calculating the distance to the moon, insisted on using astronomy for mapping. Ptolemy's contribution was to employ astronomic reckonings systematically to plot locations on a map using two coordinates—which he named latitude and longitude.

Like most learned Greeks of his day, Ptolemy was convinced that the earth was a sphere. Anyone living near a sea would have seen ships "heaving into sight." As the ship approached, its high sails always came into view first, as if the ship were coming up over the side of a hill.

Aristotle (384-322 B.C.) found additional evidence for a spherical earth in the phenomenon of the lunar eclipse, when the moon disappears behind the shadow cast by the earth: "The sphericity of the earth is proved by the evidence of our senses, for otherwise lunar eclipses would not take such forms; for ... in eclipses the dividing line is always rounded. Consequently, if the eclipse is due to the interposition of the earth, the rounded line results from a spherical shape."

Greek astronomers also knew that one star, the North Star, remained almost stationary in the night sky, whereas the other stars revolved around it in a counter-clockwise direction. This would be true if the North Star were on the axis of an immense astral sphere that rotated around a fixed earth, as Ptolemy thought (or if the North Star appears above the axis of a rotating earth, as we know today). The sphericity of the earth seemed confirmed by travelers' reports that the North Star appears higher in the sky the further north one goes. Observations of the sun told the same story: As one

OddiFacts

Gold Rush Fever

With the help of an ancient map, a mining company has struck gold—or hopes to. The Centamin Mining Company of Perth, Australia, is prospecting in Egypt by using a copy of an ancient papyrus now housed in a museum in Turin, Italy. The papyrus marks the locations of gold mines in the Sukkari region, a strip of desert 500 miles southeast of Cairo, during the reign of Seti I (1318-1304 B.C.). As yet, there is no word concerning the fortunes of Pharaoh Gold Mines, the treasure-hunting subsidiary of Centamin.

This map, 16.5 by 23 inches, now in the Biblioteca Apostolica Vaticana, was drawn in 1474 by Donnus Nicholaus Germanus, a German Benedictine monk working in Florence. Nicholaus worked from coordinates in Ptolemy's Geography, *but he also added information (about Scandinavia, for instance) not available in Ptolemy's day.*

moves north, summer days last longer and the noonday shadow cast by an upright object lengthens.

Following these clues, Greek astronomers developed a model of a spherical earth with a north-south axis, around which the heavenly sphere rotates. The sphere could be split in half at the equator to form two equal hemispheres, one northern and one southern. Ptolemy arbitrarily labeled the equator zero degrees of latitude. Since a circle has 360 degrees, the maximum degree of latitude is 90 (at the poles, one quarter of the way around the earth from the equator).

In this system, which is remarkably like our own, it only takes a simple calculation to locate a place on the earth's north-south axis: Measure the angle of the North Star above the horizon, make an adjustment, and you will know how many degrees you are above the equator. (The ancients also used other methods, such as the length of the day, to determine latitude.) Ptolemy was able to pinpoint the locations of about 400 places whose latitude was calculated by astronomic observation.

But it takes two coordinates to plot a place on a map. Cartographers need to know not only the north-south orientation (latitude) of a site but also its east-west orientation (longitude). Determining longitude proved extremely elusive—so much so that accurate calculations of longitude, especially at sea, were not made until the late 18th century.

The Greek geographers did develop a theory for determining longitude, again based on the sphericity of the earth. A complete revolution of the heavenly sphere around the earth—360 degrees—takes 24 hours; thus the sphere rotates 15 degrees every hour ($360 \div 24 = 15$). High noon, in other words, moves 15 degrees westward every hour. If, for example, Ptolemy had known that at high noon in Alexandria it is 11:00 a.m. in Carthage, he could have plotted Carthage 15 degrees to the west.

The problem is that Ptolemy had no way of knowing, at a single instant, the times of day in other places. But he did suggest an ingenious solution to the problem: If an astronomical event—such as an eclipse—could be observed simultaneously in several places, local times (with respect to high noon) could be recorded and the time differences could be used to record longitude. Ptolemy stated that this had in fact been done during a 331 B.C. lunar eclipse, observed in Carthage, North Africa, and Babylonia. But for some reason he did not make use of this information (some scholars doubt the observation was ever made). In the *Geography*, Ptolemy makes no other attempt to calculate longitude through astronomic observation. He was unable to put into practice this excellent method for determining east-west orientation. In his text, longitude is derived from estimates of distance taken from travel reports.

Ptolemy's *Geography* taught Renaissance Europe how to use latitude and longitude to chart the locations of places. This method quickly became, and has remained, standard in scientific mapmaking. Today, navigators rarely look to the sun or North Star to find their way; but even the most up-to-date navigational technologies, such as the GPS guidance systems that rely on satellite information, continue to use latitude and longitude.

Despite all these far-sighted innovations, the great Alexandrian geographer had his limitations. He had no information about equatorial and southern Africa, so he represented this area simply as *Terra Incognita*. He did not recognize that India is a peninsula, and he grossly exaggerated the size of the island of Taprobane (Sri Lanka). His representation of the Indian Ocean as an inland sea is unfortunate, since it ruins an otherwise reasonable sketch of Indochina.

One of Ptolemy's errors may even have induced Christopher Columbus to sail west. Ptolemy misjudged the circumference of the earth, assigning 50 miles to each degree; in this, he followed the North African geographer Posidonius (130-50 B.C.). Ptolemy should have used an earlier, remarkably accurate estimate by the Alexandrian mathematician Eratosthenes (270-196 B.C.) of about 70 miles to a degree, making the earth's circumference 25,200 miles. (Why Ptolemy ignored Eratosthenes is one of the mysteries of ancient science.)

This error misled explorers who were guided by Ptolemy's judgment—in particular, Columbus, who probably believed there were only 50 miles to a degree. Columbus also thought that by sailing west he would only have to go halfway around the world, 180 degrees, to reach the Asian coast. But Ptolemy had made another error: He had miscalculated the location of China. In fact, Columbus would have had to sail westward 240 degrees to reach the spice lands of the East. So Columbus believed that his journey was shorter than it really would have been. Had he known the daunting truth, would he have set sail at all?

Act One

Rush Rehm

In 1872 the young Friedrich Nietzsche burst onto the German intellectual scene by publishing *The Birth of Tragedy Out of the Spirit of Music*. Others had speculated on the origins of ancient theater, starting with Aristotle in the fourth century B.C., but no one before Nietzsche had conceived of it as a "birth," and a metaphysical one at that.

For Nietzsche, Greek tragedy was the child of a strange marriage between characteristics of the Greek gods Apollo (associated with singing, poetry and the arts) and Dionysus (the god of wine, capable of deep compassion and terrible cruelty). On the one side was the Apollonian spirit of distinct individual existence (the egoistic "dream" that each of us uniquely matters); on the other side was the Dionysian "ground-swell of Being" (those impersonal and irresistible currents of life and death, leading to oblivion). Frequently in ancient Greek tragedy, the hero dies but the chorus lives on-suggesting, to Nietzsche, the universal truth that the individual emerges only briefly, then sinks back into the all-consuming reality of the life-force, no longer capable of self-important dreams.

Whatever we think of this heady mixture of philosophy and metaphor,
Nietzsche helps us admire the ancient
Athenians for inventing an art form that
confronts unpleasant truths head-on.
Greek actors would play out such deadly
myths as the Trojan War, the murders in
the house of Atreus, Oedipus's self-inflicted
blindness, Medea's slaughter of her chil-
dren, and Pentheus's dismemberment by
his mother. In doing so, they created a
genre that has come down to us today: Not
only do we continue to attend performances of plays by Aeschylus, Sophocles and
other Greek playwrights, but many of our
theatrical forms and devices owe a direct
debt to ancient drama.

The importance of the chorus in
Greek plays points to the significant role
played by music in the development of
drama, Nietzsche's title announces. *Chorus*
is Greek for dance, and *orchestra* literally
means dancing place. The lyric form of choral poetry reminds us
that much of Greek tragedy was sung and danced, accompanied
by the music of the lyre (thus lyrical poetry).

Tragedy drew its music from daily life—songs at marriages
and funerals, songs sung while spinning and weaving, drinking
songs, work songs, specially commissioned odes for victors at
athletic contests (like the Olympic games), music for gymnastic
training and military drills, ritual shouts and incantations at

The Theater of Dionysus, on the south slope of the Athenian Acropolis, lies in a precinct that was once sacred to the god associated with wine and wild ecstasies. The theater, with its terrace of stone benches carved into the natural hillside, was first built about 500 B.C. to hold dramatic recitations from ancient poets, particularly Homer. The earliest still-visible remains date to 330 B.C.; most of the other ruins were originally built by the Romans, who enlarged the theater to hold 14,000 spectators.

OddiFacts

Aeneas in Judea?

Where would you search for the earliest manuscript of Virgil's *Aeneid*, written in the late first century B.C.? In a Roman or Pompeian library, perhaps? No, you'd have to go to Masada, in the Judean desert near the Dead Sea, where in the early 1960s Israeli archaeologist (and military commander) Yigael Yadin discovered papyrus fragments of Dido's first speech from Book IV of the epic. The original manuscript probably belonged to an officer of Rome's Tenth Legion, which had laid siege to Jewish rebels and their families in the mountain fortress during the last years of the First Jewish Revolt (66-74 A.D.) against Rome. According to the first-century A.D. Jewish historian Josephus, the rebels committed suicide rather than surrender to the Romans.

sacrifices, and hymns invoking gods. Reworked and transformed, these elements provided an important strand in the complicated weave that gave rise to tragedy (and also comedy, a genre that developed a little later).

In the earliest known theater, these lyrical-musical elements were tied to a narrative provided by Greek myths— which, for the ancient Greeks, were familiar stories passed down by oral tradition. In the mid sixth-century B.C., Athens inaugurated a contest for reciting the most famous stories at the Pan-Athenaic festival. The *Iliad, Odyssey* and other epic poems attributed to Homer were performed by a series of "rhapsodes," each of whom recited in sequence a section of the poem, accompanying himself on the lyre.

In a sense, rhapsodes were the first actors (roughly 60 percent of the *Iliad* is in direct speech), and these epic recitations provided an impetus for embodying characters fully in the new genre of theater. The addition of costumes and masks (all Greek dramatic performers wore masks) allowed actors to play several roles, eliminating the need for a narrator. For the first time, the fictional "people" of a story seemed to act out its events themselves, supplemented by a chorus (made up of citizens, household slaves or friends) caught up in the dramatic situation.

The first theatrical productions were probably also connected with the worship of the wine-god Dionysus. From paintings on vases (often wine vessels), we know that initiates in the Dionysiac cult sometimes danced around an image of the god attached to a tree or pole. These mask-like visages of Dionysus may have influenced the use of masks by actors and the chorus. Moreover, a sense of being other than, or outside of, oneself is an experience common to drinking wine and to acting a theatrical role.

The Greeks adopted Dionysus as the god of their theater, and tragic and comic performances took place at city-sponsored festivals held in his honor. The biggest festival, held at the City Dionysia (the sanctuary to Dionysus), took place every spring in Athens, where large audiences gathered over several days. The close link to Dionysus gives some support to a theory about drama's origins popular in the early 20th century. Scholars thought that the drama of the death and rebirth of Dionysus—resembling the death and rebirth of crops in winter and spring—was acted out in the earliest tragedies. (Unfortunately, however, no extant tragedy corresponds to this pattern.)

The Theater of Dionysus lies on the south slope of the Acropolis, on whose heights rose Athens's most sacred temples. Open to the sky, and looking down over the southern part of town, the theater belonged fully to the political and social world of its audience—unlike our indoor theaters, which cut off the outside world.

The beginnings of Greek theater were associated with another radical invention of the ancient Athenians: democracy. Although we find obscure references to earlier dramatists, our first secure date for tragic performances at the City Dionysia comes shortly after the expulsion from Athens of the Pisistratids—a dynasty of tyrants who ruled the city in the sixth century B.C.—and the institution of democracy in 508/507 B.C.

The tragedies themselves are profoundly concerned with social and political problems. Even while dramatizing age-old myths, they raise important civic questions: What makes a good leader? Should citizens resist illegitimate authority? How can a society develop fair laws and administer justice equitably? How should society treat women, slaves (substitute "workers") and immigrants? What can we learn from the excesses and failures of others?

We shouldn't romanticize the ancient Greeks. Athenian democracy depended in part on slave labor, and the Athenians condemned Socrates to exile or death. But they also created a form of expression that still flourishes 2,500 years later, in a world utterly different from their own. And perhaps they can help us understand that theater—along with other arts—is more than mere entertainment; it is also a means by which we might learn to integrate our social, creative and all-too-mortal lives.

... And by the People

James Sickinger

Every four years, millions of Americans, many of them united by little other than their shared citizenship, flock to schools, churches and other polling places to cast their ballots for our next president. On no other occasion do all Americans have the opportunity to vote for the same office, making presidential elections the most democratic feature of the American political system.

When we think of democracy, we usually think of the ancient Greeks, but identifying the exact origins of political practices can be tricky. Many of the city-states of the ancient Near East, for example, had popular assemblies in which citizens passed laws and elected officials. But these states are seldom labeled democracies, and our own institutions do not trace directly back to theirs.

In looking for the origins of democracy, in fact, we will not find an unbroken tradition linking the democracies of the ancient world to those of the modern age. Democratic ideals and values disappeared from western Europe during the Middle Ages, and when they resurfaced in the 17th and 18th centuries, they

OddiFacts

Tradition

Feel like eating Greek tonight? Archaion Gefsis (Ancient Tastes), a restaurant in downtown Athens, is trying to make the experience a bit more authentic. The restaurant's owners, Yannis and Suli Adamis, researched ancient recipes for two years to develop a menu that would be as close as possible to what Sophocles and Alexander actually ate. The entrées include piglet stuffed with goat liver, offal sausages and cuttlefish grilled in ink. (No sugar, tomato, rice or lemon here!) The restaurant does have its critics, however. Some point out that we cannot re-create ancient Greek cuisine with any exactitude, since we know little about the spices used. Others decry the restaurant's toga-wearing waiters (ancient Greeks wore tunics). Even so, Ancient Tastes has a loyal following, and the owners plan to open several new franchises.

were very different from their ancient predecessors. The roots of modern democracies lie in more recent times.

Nonetheless, the idea that the people should rule themselves is not new. The word "democracy," meaning "power of the people," is, of course, Greek in origin. Kingship disappeared from most of the Greek world during the so-called Dark Age (11th to 9th century B.C.). The city-states, or poleis, that began to emerge in the eighth century B.C. were not the possessions of individual rulers or even a limited number of families. These states were conceived as the common possession of their citizens and had strong egalitarian tendencies.

Just how democratic they were can be debated. The Greek city-states did not extend citizenship to all their inhabitants. Foreigners, women and slaves were excluded—a feature, however, that hardly distinguishes the ancient Greeks from other Western societies until modern times. Citizenship was limited to adult males—and not even to all of them, for full citizenship required ownership of land.

DAVID CLARK

But land ownership was not restricted to an elite few, and what made many ancient Greek city-states democratic was their large number of small farmers: These farmers had a voice, however limited, in the affairs of government.

The numbers and influence of these middling landowners is evident in Greek warfare. By the seventh century B.C., Greek armies relied on heavily armed infantrymen called hoplites. Only citizens fought as hoplites, and each hoplite provided his own spear, shield, helmet and breastplate. The widespread use of hoplite warfare implies the existence of a substantial farming class that could supply its own armor in the early Greek poleis.

Ironically, ancient Sparta—notorious for its militant authoritarianism—offers some of the earliest evidence for hoplites and their acquisition of democratic rights. Spartan citizens called themselves *homoioi*, or "equals," a name deriving from either the identical training all Spartans underwent or the equal plots of land they received (the sources are unclear). Early on these "equals" also enjoyed some power in government. The Greek biographer Plutarch (c. 46-120 A.D.) preserves a document called the Great Rhetra, supposedly from the seventh century B.C., which outlines the branches of Spartan government. It mentions two kings, a council of 30 elders and a citizen assembly with final say in all decisions. The Spartan people were their own masters.

In ancient Athens, however, democracy advanced further. The Athenians extended the rights of citizenship to a far greater portion of their male inhabitants, including the poor and landless. How and why this development occurred at Athens are questions still hotly debated among historians,* but the general outline is clear. At the start of the sixth century B.C. the reformer Solon sought to limit aristocratic oppression of the poorest Athenians by abolishing debts and debt slavery; he also ended the aristocracy's monopoly on public office and gave all citizens the right to appeal the decisions of judicial officials. In 508-507 B.C. Cleisthenes implemented further reforms that made Athenian government more representative. He reorganized the citizen body into ten tribes, each drawing citizens from different parts of Attica (the area of Greece that includes Athens), and created

*See especially Ian Morris and Kurt Raaflaub, eds., *Democracy 2500: Questions and Challenges* (Dubuque, IA: Kendall/Hunt, 1998).

a new Council of 500, which consisted of 50 members from each tribe. These reforms helped guarantee that the political process represented all Athenians.

Democracy, however, achieved its most developed state around the middle of the fifth century B.C. This final step is generally associated with a man named Ephialtes. All we know of him is that in 462-461 B.C., he sponsored reforms that deprived the Areopagus, Athens's ancient aristocratic council, of its "extra" powers and transferred them to the law courts, the Council of 500 and the assembly of adult male citizens. We do not know what powers the Areopagus had exercised previously, so we cannot say precisely what powers Ephialtes gave to the people. But from this time the popular organs of Athenian government—the Council of 500, the law courts and especially the assembly—exercised sovereign power. Subsequent years brought further advances. Eligibility for the archonship (the archon was Athens's highest public office; nine archons were appointed every year) was extended to more citizens, and public officials began to be paid for their service—which meant that more citizens could afford to participate in official political affairs.

Athenian democracy differed in many ways from our own, and we should not idealize it. The Athenians chose most of their state officials by lot (leaving the decision to chance), and most offices had a one-year term limit. These practices were designed to prevent corruption and ensured greater participation in government, but they could not have made government very efficient. The Athenians were also reluctant to extend democratic privileges to others: aliens residing in Athens had little hope of ever becoming naturalized Athenian citizens. During much of the fifth century B.C. the Athenians ruled over many other

Greek city-states, including former allies; the tribute exacted from these cities helped to pay public officials in democratic Athens. It is no exaggeration to suggest, as many historians have, that democracy and imperialism were quite closely connected.

Still, one Athenian practice may have contemporary relevance. At the end of the fifth century B.C., the Athenians began to pay citizens to attend meetings of the assembly. Originally the first 6,000 to show up for a meeting received the small amount of one obol (not even half a day's wage), but by the middle of the fourth century B.C. that payment had grown six fold. Were the Athenians on to something? When voter turnout in American presidential elections hovers near 50 percent, this may be one lesson we wish to take from our Athenian ancestors.

The Verdict Is ...

Alan L. Boegehold

We usually picture jurors as 12 duly sworn, impaneled citizens, with one of them standing up at the end of a trial to deliver a verdict. Indeed the word "juror" is cognate with the Latin word *iurare*, meaning to swear, and it implies an oath to judge truly. But where in the Western world did the notion of such judging groups originate?

In Homer's *Iliad*, Book 18, the god Hephaistos creates a new shield for Achilles. On that shield, he blazons a whole world along with scenes of war and peace—a tableau that might well have been common in the early eighth-century B.C. Hellenic world in which Homer lived. One scene takes place in a market, where two men are in fierce disagreement after a killing. They then submit their dispute to what scholars normally interpret as a jury trial: "The people were cheering for both, on the part of one side and the other. The heralds kept the people in order, and the elders sat on shaped stones in a consecrated circle. They held in their hands the batons of loud-voiced heralds with which they would rise and speak the right

in turn. Two talents of gold lay in their midst to give to him among them who spoke the straightest right."

If there are jurors here, however, they are present only in the most schematic way. No one is sworn. The crowd does not seem to do the judging, unless they determine who delivers the straightest verdict. Elders rise and speak, but it is not entirely clear what they say.

Nevertheless, the Homeric passage does suggest how the concept of judging arose: Communities likely established systems of impartial judges to keep vendettas from developing. When men went about armed and ready to defend their honor, even trivial quarrels could turn violent. If someone was killed, blood had to be paid for blood shed—and the cycle of vengeance went on. Only by reaching civil agreements, by allowing third parties to resolve disputes, could this be obviated.

At Athens, possibly by the time of Solon (early sixth century B.C.), and certainly by the fifth century, citizens were chosen by lot and sworn to render impartial verdicts in cases ranging from

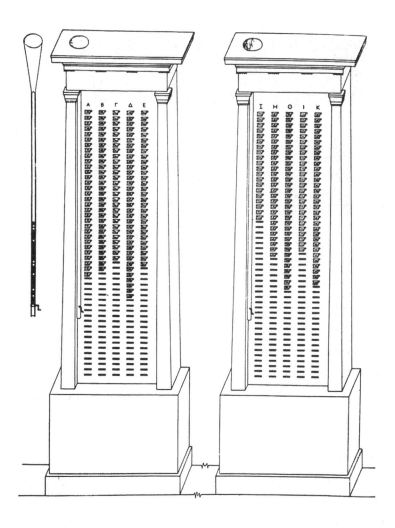

Potential Athenian jurors were divided into ten groups, each designated by one of the first ten letters of the Greek alphabet. They were then given small bronze identification tags, called pinakia *(opposite), inscribed with the juror's letter. Two allotment machines, or* kleroteria, *each with five columns, were also marked with the first ten letters of the alphabet. Balls released into the machines determined which jurors were released for the day and which jurors were to serve.*

OddiFacts

What's in a Name?

When you hear a news report delivered by Sandor Vanocur, you are experiencing the eternal influence of Alexander the Great (356-323 B.C.). Evidence of Alexander's greatness can be found in the enduring popularity of his name throughout Asia Minor, Russia, Europe, the Indian subcontinent and the English-speaking world. Russian Alexandrs, Saschas and Sandels; Muslim Iskanders; German-Yiddish Senders, Sandors and Sand'ls; Spanish Alejandros; and English Alexanders and Alecs continue to pay linguistic tribute to the Macedonian warrior-king.

money disputes to capital crimes. The jurors sat in panels of 500, 1,000, 1,500 or, on one occasion, 6,000. Called *dikastai*, or "judges" in Greek, their collective opinion was final. In effect, they represented the will of the city itself, and there could be no tribunal superior to that.

Aristophanes's comedy *Wasps*—whose central character is a rascally juror bent on doing harm—suggests how these panels were organized in the late fifth century B.C. According to the play (with help from scholars who lived in the centuries after Aristophanes), jurors were sworn en masse once a year at Ardettos Hill in Athens. On trial days, after listening to both the prosecution and the defense, the jurors voted by dropping a pebble into one of two urns, one for acquittal and one for conviction. A simple majority determined the verdict, with a tie going to the defendant.

By the late fifth century B.C. jurors were even paid for their labors. They received three obols a day, about the wage paid to an artisan for a day's labor at a public building or temple.

The Athenians devised a new—and far more formal—system in the early fourth century B.C.E. To be eligible, potential jurors had to be male, at least 30 years old and free of public debt. The jury pool was divided into ten sections, each labeled by one of the first ten letters of the alphabet, from alpha to kappa. Each juror was given a small bronze identification tag, called a *pinakion*, inscribed with the juror's letter, his father's name and his place of residence.

As we know from various speeches of fourth-century orators, the *dikastai* took an oath that went more or less as follows: "I shall vote according to the laws and decrees, but when laws do not exist I shall use my best judgment. I shall vote concerning those things that are at issue, but I shall listen impartially to both accusation and defense."

Aristotle's *Constitution of the Athenians* (c. 330 B.C.) gives an account of how jurors were chosen, situated and paid—and much of this has now been confirmed by archaeology. Excavations of the Athenian Agora by the American School of Classical Studies at Athens have uncovered court buildings and paraphernalia used in the administration of justice. One thing we learn from Aristotle and archaeology: The Athenians took extraordinary (and complicated) steps to prevent corruption in the courts.

In the Agora were several court buildings, which were kept separate from the temptations of the marketplace by a fence with ten entrances, one for each of the ten tribes of Athens. (These tribal affiliations are not to be confused with the ten-letter system; members of the same tribe would randomly be assigned different letters.) Outside each entrance stood two *kleroteria*, or allotment machines, used for choosing jurors. Each *kleroterion* contained five columns of slots, and each column was marked with one of the first ten letters of the Greek alphabet—alpha to epsilon on one machine, and zeta to kappa on the other. The jurors would gather at their tribal entrance and drop their *pinakia* into one of ten chests labeled with their letter—alpha *pinakia* were placed in a chest labeled "alpha," betas in the beta chest, and so on to kappa. A magistrate then randomly picked one *pinakion* from each chest. The men to whom these *pinakia* belonged were now jurors for the day. In addition, they were to carry out the next step by removing the rest of the *pinakia* from their chest and plugging them into the slots of the *kleroterion* column marked with their letter.

A magistrate then shook up black and white balls in a terracotta vessel and poured them into a funnel-shaped opening at the top of the *kleroterion* that led by means of a pipe to the bottom of the *kleroterion*. One ball at a time was released. If the ball was black, the jurors whose *pinakia* were plugged into that row were released; if the ball was white, the jurors in that row were to serve in a trial that day.

The allotted jurors retrieved their *pinakia* and entered the trial precinct. As they passed through the entrance, they were given a randomly drawn token naming the court they were to serve in that day. The jurors handed their *pinakia* to a magistrate, who deposited them in a chest specially designated for their court (as noted on the token). The jurors then proceeded to their court, where they received another token assigning them seats.

All these elaborate precautions were to safeguard fairness. Since judging panels had hundreds of jurors, any concentration of like-minded jurors who wanted to make noise could seriously compromise the judicial process.

A trial began with a speech by the citizen who initiated the action, followed by the defense. Litigants were expected to speak on their own behalf—though they could reserve some time for others to testify for them. Prosecution and defense had equal time, monitored by a *klepsydra*, or water-clock, and trials could last no longer than a day. The jurors voted immediately after hearing the speeches, apparently without deliberating among themselves. They were given two small bronze disks, each with a short axle projecting from its center. These disks were identical except for the axles—on one ballot the axle was solid (for acquittal), whereas on the other it was hollow (for conviction). The jurors simply dropped the ballot that counted into one amphora and the invalid ballot into a discard amphora. Finally, the jurors were given back their *pinakia* as they were called forth to receive their pay. When the ballots were counted, a simple majority determined the verdict. Ties favored the defendant

This is all very familiar. Ordinary folk, without special training or learned instruction, making decisions about fellow citizens' lives and fortunes. In ancient Greece as in modern America, juries are a powerful cohering and monitoring force, insuring that justice be rendered impartially—that is, that justice be blind.

On the Pill

George B. Griffenhagen

As soon as man began to write, it seems, he was giving medical advice. Prescriptions and formulas are plentiful in the literature of ancient Mesopotamia. One cuneiform tablet suggests the following for an undisclosed ailment: "Pulverize the seed of the carpenter plant, the gum resin of the markasi plant, and thyme; dissolve in beer; let the man drink."

Mesopotamian medicaments, however effective, are all liquid preparations. The Sumerians, Babylonians and Assyrians apparently knew nothing of what is for us the most common kind of dosage: the pill.

The earliest-known reference to pills comes in Egyptian medical papyri from the second millennium B.C. The most complete medical document is the so-called Ebers Papyrus, which was acquired in Luxor in 1869 by an American adventurer named Edwin Smith, who then sold it to the German Egyptologist Georg Ebers. In 1875 Ebers published a facsimile edition of the 110-page-long papyrus scroll, which dates to the ninth year of the reign of Pharaoh Amenophis I (1525-1504 B.C.).

The Ebers Papyrus describes 811 formulas for medicines used in ancient Egypt. Although the exact identity of the substances mentioned in the papyrus is often a matter of conjecture, we learn that the drugs were boiled and strained or pounded in a stone mortar. Remedies were often given as potions with beer, wine from grapes or dates, or milk. Sometimes they were formed into candy with honey, or baked into cakes with grease. But the ancient Egyptians also invented pills: "Malachite is ground fine, put into bread dough, made into three pills, and gulped down with sweet beer," the Ebers Papyrus instructs.

It was the Greeks and Romans who popularized the pill, creating the tablets and lozenges we know today. The most common form of medication in ancient Greece was the *katapotium*, which means "something to be swallowed." It initially referred to a soft preparation made by mixing medicinal substances and other ingredients in a semi-liquid form. However, this preparation was often so unpleasant to swallow that the Greeks created lozenges, which were taken with wine or water. Henceforth, *katapotium* referred to a pill.

Greek physicians didn't prescribe aspirin and rest. They said, "Take a *katapotium* the size of a bean!" In the first century A.D., the Roman writer Aulus Cornelius Celsus advised readers to take *katapotia* the size of an almond or an Egyptian bean. Others prescribed *katapotia* the size of a dried pea. When a pill got very large, it was called a *bolos*, meaning "lump." Of course, *bolos* is the ancestor of our "bolus," which carries exactly the same meaning today: a large pill that is hard to swallow.

In his *Natural History*, Pliny the Elder (23-79 A.D.) refers to pills not as a *katapotia* but as *pilulae* ("little balls"), from which our word derives. Greco-Roman physicians widely prescribed a

Using mortars, pestles and other equipment, a woman pharmacist and her assistant produce medicines and ointments in their medicina, *a shop where drugs were made and sold in the ancient Roman Empire. This second-century A.D. Roman relief is in the National Museum of Antiquities in Saint-Germain en Laye, France.*

OddiFacts

Dr. Spock He's Not

The second-century B.C. physician Demastes, like other educated Greeks, thought that the human fetus developed from the male sperm. Demastes, however, took the idea further, developing a mathematical theory of the development of human infants. In a normal nine-month pregnancy, the sperm turns to foam (after 6 days), blood (after 15 days) and flesh (after 27 days). After 45 days, this fleshy creature begins to take shape. The baby moves at 90 days and is born at 250 days. "It's really a form of cooking," says Holt Parker, a classics professor at the University of Cincinnati who translated Demastes's text. Four paragraphs of Demastes's *The Care of Pregnant Women* are quoted in an 11th-century A.D. manuscript, recently rediscovered in a library in Florence, Italy. This is all we know of Demastes, other than a reference to his discussion of babies' diets by his contemporary Ceranus.

medication called Pilula Cochina, containing aloes and a strong purgative like colocynth (bitter apple).

One of the most popular medicines sold by drug vendors in Greece and Rome was *hiera picra* (holy bitters), for treating upset stomachs. According to tradition, it was first used in temples of Asclepius, the Greek god of medicine. Over the centuries, physicians altered and added ingredients to the formula, sometimes attaching their names to the compound.

The earliest recorded formula for *hiera picra* is that of Themison of Laodicea, in western Anatolia, a physician who practiced in Rome under Augustus (31 B.C.-14 A.D.). His recipe consists of aloes mixed with "mastic, saffron, Indian nard [probably spikenard], carpobalsamum and asarum [a wild ginger], of each an ounce." Owing to the nauseous taste, the preparation was made into a bolus.

The first-century A.D. physician Scribonius Largus records that wealthy Romans were offering large sums of money for a bitters called Hiera Pachii. This medication had been developed (and kept secret) by a

man named Pachius, the personal physician of the Roman emperor Tiberius (14-37 A.D.). The secret formula was subsequently discovered in a manuscript Pachius had dedicated to Tiberius, and the emperor promptly passed the formula on to Scribonius, with instructions that it should be published. This pill consisted of 14 herbs and became known as Hiera Scribonius Largus.

The famous physician Galen of Pergamum (c. 129-199 A.D.), who began as a gladiator and ended up as court physician to the Roman emperor Marcus Aurelius (161-180 A.D.), was a firm believer in the efficacy of *hiera picra* and invented his own formula: Hiera Galeni. It consisted of "Socotrine aloes 100 parts, cinnamon or canella, spikenard, xylobalsam, mastic, asarum, and saffron, six parts of each, and sufficient honey to make it into an electuary or pilula."

Ancient pharmacists used the bronze spatulas shown above to roll out a pill mass in the grooves of the 3-inch-long pill machine at left, which is from either Cyprus or Rhodes. They would then slice the long cylindrical pill mass into pills with the spatula.

101

The practice of "trademarking" medications is recorded as early as 500 B.C. Pills known as *terra sigillata* (sealed earth, not to be confused with the pottery of the same name) were prepared from clay found on the Aegean island of Lemnos. The clay was dug up, formed into discs and impressed with an identifying seal while still soft. The first seal used was an image of a goat, because the mixture contained Lemnos clay and goat's blood. In time, the digging of Lemnos clay became associated with the worship of the goddess Diana that took place on the sixth of May; henceforth an image of Diana was used as the seal.

The first-century A.D. Greek physician Pedanius Dioscorides prescribed Lemnos earth as a treatment for dysentery, internal ulcers, hemorrhages, gonorrhea, fevers and kidney problems. *Terra sigillata* has its counterparts even today in earthy compounds of magnesium, aluminum and silicon (like kaolin and bentonite, used to treat diarrhea).

The Romans used small rectangular slabs to make pills, and they often carried their pill slabs with them to distant parts of the Roman Empire. Two slabs in the Archaeological Museum at Namur, in Belgium, are made of black marble and measure about 4 inches by 3 inches. Greek and Roman medical authorities also frequently mention bronze or copper spatulas, which they used to roll the pill mass and cut it into pills. The spatula still serves as an essential tool of the modern pharmacist.

The Romans also employed the first pill machine. A 3-inch-long rectangular stone from ancient Cyprus or Rhodes, now in the British Museum, is carved with a number of grooves on one side. These grooves apparently served as pipes in which the pill mass was rolled and cut into pills.

Coating pills to make them palatable was practiced by the Arabs, who absorbed much Greco-Roman medical learning. One famous Arab physician, Abu Bakr Muhammad ibn Zakariya al-Razi (c. 850-925 A.D.), known in the west as Rhazes, recommended covering pills with a coating made from edible seeds. Another physician, Abu Ali al-Husayn ibn Abd Allah ibn Sina (980-1037), or Avicenna, suggested that pills be silvered or gilded—not simply to mask bad taste, but to employ the supposed medicinal effects of silver and gold.

The Arabs passed these techniques on to the West along with their rich knowledge of drugs. When the early 17th-century Parisian pharmacist Jean de Renou recommended that pills with a bitter taste should be gilded or coated with powdered spices, he was drawing directly on Arab learning. Well into the 19th century, pills were still being coated with gold and silver, though by this time pharmacists had begun to warn people that gilded pills often passed through the alimentary canal without being digested, owing to their metallic covering.

Today's pharmaceutical industry produces millions of pills (mostly in the form of tablets and capsules) each day—a reminder of our immense debt to ancient Egypt, Greece and Rome.

A Codex Moment

Timothy Rogers

My daughter Delia is mastering language at a frightening rate. At 15 months, she understood the word "two" and said "mailman" when our dogs barked. Even then, she was using language to categorize objects: "Duck," for instance, meant anything resembling a bird, and "choo-choo" meant all large vehicles as well as the laundry baskets we sometimes used as wagons.

When Delia first used the word "book," she was referring to materials that appear in the form of a codex (a collection of leaves or pages bound at one side). Such bound volumes have come to represent everyone's image of a book. But codices were not, and are not, the only form a text can take.

In the 18th century B.C., Hammurabi's law code was inscribed on a 7-foot-high chunk of basalt. More than a thousand years earlier, the Sumerians were keeping financial records on clay tablets and inscribing text on small seals made of seashell or gemstones.

For lengthy, portable documents, however, another medium was needed. The Torah, an integral part of any synagogue, reminds us that when the ancients referred to a book, they usually meant a scroll (also called a roll). Scrolls were made of several materials. Some are cured animal skins; a tiny seventh-century B.C. scroll (one and a half inches long and a half inch wide), found in a tomb in Jerusalem and inscribed with text from the "Priestly Blessing" (Numbers 6:24-26), is made of silver; and one of the Dead Sea Scrolls is copper.

The material preferred by ancient Egyptians and Greeks was papyrus, a tall marsh plant that grows abundantly in the Nile Valley. Sheets were made by placing layers of papyrus strips at right angles to one another and then pounding or pressing them flat; the sap would then bind the strips together. Rolls were formed by attaching papyrus sheets end to end. Ancient scribes generally wrote in columns parallel to the short side of the scroll rather than down the entire length of the scroll (which could be 30 feet long for a Greek scroll and three times that for an Egyptian papyrus). The reader would peruse the text by unrolling one end of the scroll and rolling up the other.

Versions of the codex may have been used by the Mesopotamians early in the second millennium B.C. These early codices were wood, clay or ivory writing tablets, with two or more leaves joined by hinges or leather thongs. Many of the writing tablets had hollowed-out surfaces that were coated with wax and marked up with a stylus; the surface could then be smoothed over so that new text could be inscribed. These multi-leaved wax tablets were suited only for short writings, such as private letters or inventory lists.

In this frontispiece of an eighth-century copy of the sixth-century Latin translation of the Bible, Codex Grandior, *by* Cassiodorus, *the prophet Ezra writes in a codex. The shelves hold Cassiodorus's nine-volume edition of the Bible, the* Codex Novices, *and a copy of St. Jerome's* Vulgate *rests at the prophet's feet.*

OddiFacts

Shhhh!

Reading out loud was the norm in the ancient world. Plutarch notes that when Alexander the Great (336-323 B.C.) stood before his troops and silently perused a letter from his mother, his soldiers were bewildered. They had never seen anyone read without vocalizing the words. Julius Caesar's aide-de-camp thought his boss was experiencing an epileptic seizure as he quietly studied a document. Silent reading was still considered an oddity in 384 A.D., when Augustine, then a young professor of Latin rhetoric, marveled at how Ambrose of Milan (later canonized, as was Augustine) read: "His eyes scanned the page ... but his voice was silent and his tongue was still" (*Confessions* 6.3). In the semi-literate world of antiquity, reading was viewed as a public, not a private, affair. Indeed, the lack of word separations and arbitrary line wraps in inscriptions almost demanded that readers verbalize words to make sense of them.

Two things combined to facilitate the western world's transition from the scroll to the kind of codex that, today, we call a book: the development of parchment (the cured skins of sheep, goats or cattle) as a viable alternative to papyrus, and the rise of Christianity. According to the first-century A.D. Roman historian Pliny the Elder, parchment came into use as a result of competition between Ptolemy V (210-180 B.C.) of Egypt and Eumenes II (197-159 B.C.) of Pergamum, in western Anatolia. Seeking to maintain the Alexandria Library's preeminence in the ancient world, Ptolemy banned the export of papyrus to be used at the library of Pergamum, forcing Eumenes to develop a new writing material. Whether or not the story is true, Pergamum was an important exporter of parchment (the word "parchment" derives from the name "Pergamum"), and an important competition was developing between the two writing surfaces.

Parchment had several advantages over papyrus. It was available wherever there were sheep, goats or cattle. It was more durable than papyrus, which the Greeks complained lasted only two or three centuries (some ancient Egyptian papyri have survived because of the dry Egyptian climate, not because of the strength of the material). Parchment could be scraped clean and reused—creating a palimpsest—more successfully than papyrus. And parchment could be folded, quired (one sheet stuffed inside another, like this book) and bound. Papyrus, which was also used in codices for several centuries, was weakened by folding and sewing.

The codex form itself provided distinct benefits. The leaves of codices, whatever material they were made of, could be inscribed on both sides, whereas scrolls were generally written on only one side. Even more importantly, codices could be referred to more easily than scrolls. To find a passage in a scroll, the reader needed to unroll the document to reach the proper citation; with a codex, one needed only to turn pages. Finally, codices were simply easier to carry around and read. The first-century A.D. Roman poet Martial praised parchment codices in his Epigrams: "You, who wish my poems should be everywhere with you, and look to have them as companions on a long journey, buy these which the parchment confines in small pages. Assign your book-boxes to the great; this copy of me one hand can grasp."

Despite Martial's praise, the ancient Romans must not have had a pressing need for the parchment codex. Wall paintings and library caches from Pompeii and Herculaneum show that the Romans continued to use scrolls in the first century A.D. Early Christians, however, needed everything a parchment or papyrus codex could provide. The codex's size, portability and ease of reference—together with the fact that it was not yet associated with the major texts of pagan writers—made the form ideal for an underground religion based on a written text.

The bibliographer Leila Avrin has pointed out that all extant Christian works from second-century A.D. Egypt are codices, whereas only two percent of the surviving non-Christian manuscripts are codical in form.* Indeed, many of the oldest and best-preserved parchment codices, such as the early fourth-century Codex Sinaiticus, found at St. Catherine's Monastery in the Sinai, and the mid-fourth-century Codex Vaticanus in the Vatican Library, contain early editions of the New Testament. As Christianity spread, so did the codex. By the time Constantine the Great granted Christians complete religious freedom in 313, the codex had essentially replaced the scroll except in certain official functions.

The dominance of papyrus as a writing material faded along with the scroll, although more slowly. The fourth-century Gnostic Gospels found in Nag Hammadi, Egypt, in 1945, for instance, are papyrus codices. But in the end, the more flexible, durable parchment codex won the day. Clearly, we have not completely abandoned the rolled book. Many large books and most magazines are printed in columns, a format that harkens back to ancient rolls. And when we need to see the next block of information on our computers, we don't turn the pages, we "scroll" down.

Nonetheless, when we think of a book, we think of a codex. Delia knows this. Seeing a roll of paper, she doesn't compare it to her copy of *Mr. Brown Can Moo! Can You?* She holds it to her lips and yells "Toot, toot!"

---

* Leila Avrin, *Scribes, Scripts and Books: The Book Arts from Antiquity to the Renaissance* (The British Library, 1991), p. 174.

Fixing the Millennium

Leonora Neville

Most of us are already familiar with the Common Era (C.E.) as a secular version of the *Anno Domini* (A.D.) chronological system, which dates events according to "the Year of Our Lord," or the birth of Jesus. But when exactly did people start dating things from the time of Christ?

Obviously when Jesus was born no one had a calendar saying it was year 0. Herod had no way of knowing he came to power in the year 37 B.C. In fact, it was not until hundreds of years after the time of Jesus that anyone tried to reckon the years that had elapsed since his birth.

Most of the earliest Christians were converted Jews, who relied on the Jewish lunar calendar. As Christianity spread to other groups, however, most people continued to use the Roman calendar introduced by Julius Caesar in 46 B.C. (Before Christ). Created with the help of the Alexandrian astronomer Sosigenes, Caesar's "Julian" calendar formally established a solar year measuring 12 months or 365¼ days. (The quarter was made up in an extra day every fourth or "leap" year.)

While the Julian Calendar effectively standardized the length of the year throughout the Roman Empire—and made it easy to refer to a particular date within a given year—a variety of options were still available for distinguishing one year from another. The Romans frequently referred to a particular year by the names of the consuls who had ruled at the time. Roman historians sometimes also numbered years from "the founding of the city of Rome" (*ab urbe condita*) in what we would call 753 B.C. A third way of numbering years was by fixing them in relation to the Indiction, or 15-year tax cycle.

In the fourth century A.D., many Christians began situating themselves within the "Era of the Martyrs," which started in 284 A.D. with the Roman emperor Diocletian's persecution of Christians. Citizens of Antioch in Syria pegged "year 1" to 49 B.C. in commemoration of Julius Caesar's dictatorship. In the fifth century many Greek-speaking Christians started to number years from the creation of the world (*Anno Mundi*), which they believed occurred in either 5493 or 5509 B.C. By the tenth century A.D., *Anno Mundi* dating—with the world's creation fixed at 5509 B.C.—became standard in the Byzantine Empire and hence in the Orthodox countries of Eastern Europe.

The first person to number years from the birth of Jesus was a little-known scholar and abbot named Dionysius Exiguus (Dennis the Little), who lived in Rome in the sixth century A.D. When the church timetable used for calculating the correct date of Easter was about to run out, the Pope asked Dionysius to extend it. Finding the exact date of Easter was always problematic for church officials because they relied on the Roman solar calendar, whereas the anniversary of Christ's death and resurrection were supposed to take place after the Passover festival, which was grounded on the Jewish lunar calendar. While figuring out the chronological details for his Easter table, Dionysius counted backwards and established what he thought was the year of the birth or "Incarnation" of Christ. (He was off by at least four years. Modern scholars think that Jesus was actually born between 7 and 4 B.C.) Dionysius used his chronology to label the then-current year *Anno Domini Nostri Jesu Christi* (the Year of Our Lord Jesus Christ) 532.

Dionysius's invention did not spread like wildfire. Even Dionysius did not use it all the time. The greatest advocate of the A.D. dating system was the great English churchman and historian, the Venerable Bede (673-735). Bede systematically used A.D. to describe the whole history of England. His history was very influential in Europe and his style of dating started to be used in French-speaking regions in the eighth century and in Germany in the ninth century. The Catholic Church was not in the vanguard of the *Anno Domini* system, but used both A.D. dates and the regnal years of the Popes until the 15th century.

OddiFacts

Pontifications

Why is the pope, the head of the Roman Catholic Church, referred to as the pontiff? That term derives from the Latin word *pontifex*, or bridge-builder, suggesting the papal role as mediator between God and man. In ancient times, Roman emperors assumed the title Pontifex Maximus, thus declaring themselves not only the political head of state but also the chief priest of Rome. The bridge-building metaphor, obviously an apt image of a united heaven and earth, would have had special meaning for Roman citizens—since Roman engineers built actual concrete and stone bridges over rivers all around the known world. In Rome alone, six ancient bridges still span the Tiber River.

$24 \times 60 = 1446 \div 11.25 = 128$

While the A.D. system spread throughout Europe during the Middle Ages, the basic calendar in use was still Julius Caesar's. But the Julian calendar's reckoning of 365¼ days in one solar year was too long by 11 minutes and 14 seconds each year. This meant that over time astronomical phenomena fell out of sync with their fixed dates in the calendar. By the 16th century, the spring equinox occurred ten days before March 21!

In the 1570s a group of church astronomers, led by the Jesuit scholar Christopher Clavius, recalculated the length of the solar year and arrived at a more precise estimate of 365.2422 days. (Their estimate was remarkably accurate; modern scientists calculate the year as 365.242199 days.) Since the difference between the Jesuit solar year (365.242 days) and the Julian year (365.25 days) added up to a total of 3.12 days every 400 years, the Jesuits proposed that three out of every four centennial years should no longer be leap years. (For example, the centennial years 1700, 1800 and 1900 were not leap years, but the year 2000 will be one.) This modification to the Julian system saves three days every four centuries and ensures that the modern calendar loses only .0003 days each year.

In 1582, Pope Gregory XIII issued a papal bull officially adopting the Jesuit calendar reforms. To eliminate the already existing time lag between astronomical phenomena and their fixed dates, he also cut ten days out of October that year. By papal decree, October 4 was followed by October 15, 1582.

Unfortunately, Gregory's reforms were ill-timed. At the moment of his decree, much of Europe was embroiled in the Wars of Religion (1562-1598) and a good many people in Europe (to say nothing of the rest of the world) were unwilling to change their calendars just because the Pope said so. While the new Gregorian calendar was adopted fairly quickly by the Catholic countries of Europe, the German Protestant nations refused to accept Gregory's reforms until 1699. England clung to the Julian calendar until 1752!

With the onset of Western colonization and increased international trade, the Gregorian calendar started to gain a foothold in non-Western countries in the late 19th century. Japan was the first Asian country to adopt it in 1873. The upheavals of the First World War accelerated the process, with most eastern European and East Asian countries falling into line between 1912 and 1918. Greece—and the Eastern Orthodox Church—eventually also adopted a modified version of the Gregorian calendar in 1923.

Of course, all of this leads us to one final question. If we're numbering years according to the life of Jesus, why don't we celebrate New Year's Eve with Christ's birth on December 25, or with the date of his conception on March 25 (which also coincides with the arrival of Spring)? As it happened, both of these dates were popular days for celebrating the beginning of the New Year throughout the Middle Ages. January 1 only became universally recognized as New Year's Day with the general adoption of the Gregorian calendar. So if you can't find a baby sitter for December 31, you can always celebrate on March 25. And if you're sick of the whole thing you could use Byzantine time and say it's *Anno Mundi* 7511.